P9-DGX-588

BO
KNOWS
BO

Bo Jackson

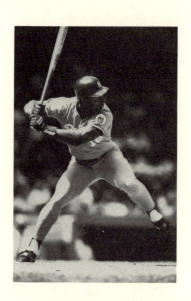

The Autobiography
of a Ballplayer

BO
KNOWS
BO

BO JACKSON
and
Dick Schaap

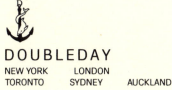

DOUBLEDAY

NEW YORK   LONDON
TORONTO   SYDNEY   AUCKLAND

PUBLISHED BY DOUBLEDAY
a division of Bantam Doubleday
Dell Publishing Group, Inc., 666 Fifth Avenue,
New York, New York 10103

DOUBLEDAY and the portrayal of an anchor with a dolphin
are trademarks of Doubleday, a division of Bantam
Doubleday Dell Publishing Group, Inc.

"The Monster in the Mirror." Copyright © 1989 Splotched Animal Music
(BMI) and Sesame Street, Inc. (ASCAP). Words and Music by Christopher Cerf
and Norman Stiles. Reprinted by permission.

Excerpt from "At Bessemer" from *A Walk with Tom Jefferson* by Philip Levine.
Copyright © 1988 by Philip Levine. Reprinted by permission of
Alfred A. Knopf, Inc.

Title page photo of Baseball Bo by Tom DiPace.
Title page photo of Football Bo by Robert Hagan/AllSport USA.

Library of Congress Cataloging-in-Publication Data

Jackson, Bo, 1962–
Bo knows Bo : the autobiography of a ballplayer / by Bo Jackson
and Dick Schaap.
p. cm.
1. Jackson, Bo, 1962–   . 2. Baseball players—United States—
Biography. 3. Football players—United States—Biography.
I. Schaap, Dick, 1934–   II. Title.
GV865.J28A3 1990
796'.092—dc20
[B]   90-41073
CIP
ISBN 0-385-41620-2

Copyright © 1990 by Bo Jackson and Dick Schaap
"Bo Jackson: An Appreciation by George Brett"
Copyright © 1990 by George Brett
"Bo Jackson: An Appreciation by Howie Long"
Copyright © 1990 by Howie Long
All Rights Reserved
Printed in the United States of America

DESIGN: Stanley S. Drate/Folio Graphics Co., Inc.

November 1990

2 4 6 8 10 11 9 7 5 3

This book is for the only person I know who is stronger than I am—and more stubborn. My mom. When I was growing up, she cleaned people's houses during the day and cleaned a motel at night. She also raised ten children.

And people try to tell me that playing two sports is hard.

—BO JACKSON
1990

BO JACKSON: AN APPRECIATION BY GEORGE BRETT

Bo Jackson is my hero.

Isn't that ridiculous?

Bo was in elementary school when I joined the Kansas City Royals and he was in junior high when I won my first batting championship and he was in high school when I hit .390 in 1980—and he's my hero.

It's ridiculous, but it's true.

I would give anything to be in his body for one day—just to see what it's like. What it's like to run that fast. What it's like to hit a ball that far. What it's like to throw a ball that hard.

When he's at the top of his game, it's a sight to see. It's beyond your wildest dreams. It's beyond *my* wildest dreams.

Everybody has a favorite Bo home run. I've seen him hit them into the upper deck at Tiger Stadium and into the monuments at Yankee Stadium, into places where no mortal is supposed to hit a ball. But my favorite is one he hit in 1987, his first full season with the Royals.

Bo came up with the bases loaded, Snell pitching for Detroit, Nathaniel Snell, a right-hander who threw hard, had a good slider, a little sinker. I was on second base, and I could see the pitch Snell threw Bo. A slider three or four inches off the plate, down and away. Bo reached out and hit it off the end of his bat. He didn't get good wood on it. Broke his bat. And he hit it into the waterfall in right-center field in Royals Stadium, 420 feet away.

I've been playing in Royals Stadium for seventeen years, and I bet I've hit six, maybe seven home runs into the waterfall, and that's where my power is, right-center field. Bo went opposite field and hit a broken-bat, 420-foot home run—and this was in the middle of April, when it's cold and the ball doesn't travel well.

He's awesome in the field, too. Early this season, we were playing the Chicago White Sox in Kansas City, and Carlton Fisk was on first, Carlos Martinez at bat. Martinez hit a ball into left-center field, the kind of ball you look at and say, "Aw, man," because you know it's going up the alley, and Bo just put his head down and ran and, at the last second, turned around and threw his glove up and caught the ball at the 385-foot sign.

Fisk was already at second base, thinking there was no way Bo could catch the ball. Bo, running full speed, put his foot up against the wall, bounced off, pivoted and, without even taking a step, threw a one-hopper that was no more than five feet off line, five feet up toward home plate. I was playing first and I took the throw and dove at Fisk, who was diving for the bag, and I tagged him, doubling him up. It was crazy. Fisk walked off shaking his head; he didn't believe it.

Bo made the same kind of impossible play in Seattle last year. Harold Reynolds was on first base, tenth inning, score tied, Scott Bradley at bat. Reynolds was running on the pitch, and Bradley hit the ball down the left-field line, into the corner, extra bases, and as fast as Reynolds is, I figured, "That's it, the game's over. He's going to score easy." But Bo grabbed the ball at the warning track, turned and threw home—more than 300 feet away—on the fly. A rocket. Bob Boone was catching, and Boonie told me afterward his mind just went—*click-click-click*—from "We don't have a chance," to "*Maybe* we have a chance," to "Holy shit, we got him!" When Reynolds saw the replay the next day, he still didn't believe it.

I've watched Bo play football, too. He's made me a Raiders fan. I try to go to every home game. I stood on the sidelines and saw him score his first touchdown in the National Football League, a 35-yard run against the Denver Broncos. At the thirty, Mike Harden, then with the Broncos, now with the Raiders, set himself to stop Bo, and Bo just lowered his head and ran through Harden, leveled him, knocked him into another world. I was on the sidelines, too, when Bo went 92 yards for a touchdown against Cincinnati last year, making him the first player in the history of the NFL to run more than 90 yards for touchdowns *twice* in a career. If Bo ever concentrated on football, I think he'd break all the running records.

I think Bo could win the Indianapolis 500. I think he could knock out Mike Tyson. I think he could win the U.S. Open—tennis or golf, either one. I really think if he set his mind to anything, athletically, he could do it. He's just the best athlete I've ever seen.

That body is beyond belief. I've been in lots of NFL locker rooms, and I've seen some muscular men, linebackers and running backs, but nothing compares to Bo. I almost take him for granted now, but when he first came up to the Royals, I've got to admit, I used to sneak looks at him walking around the locker room in nothing but a jockstrap. All I could think was "What do I have to do to get a body like that? Give up bread for a month? Swear off beer? I'll do it."

The other thing that's remarkable is that Bo's success hasn't gone to his head. It really hasn't. All the money he's got, all the talent, all the fame, all the attention, it doesn't affect him. And he gets the kind of attention every day that I got for a couple of months the year I almost hit .400. I'm lying. He gets more. People come to the ballpark just to see him taking batting practice. When we walk into a restaurant together, I might as well be invisible. I've been in the big leagues seventeen years, and nobody notices me. Everybody's going, "Bo! Bo! Bo!" I'm going, "Bo! Bo! Bo!" too.

Bo is a family man. You get a lot of guys in sports, their families are there, but that's not what's number one. With Bo, his wife and his kids are number one.

I'm proud to be on the same team with Bo. When he was a rookie, I got him to give me a picture of him standing with the Heisman Trophy, and I kept it over my locker for three years.

I've never asked him for an autograph, but I'm going to. Before I quit, I'm going to get him to autograph a baseball for me and autograph a football for me and give me one of his bats. I'm going to save them, and when I finally settle down and have children, when I'm sixty or seventy, and my children ask me what I used to do for a living, I'll tell them, "I played baseball. I played with Bo Jackson."

—GEORGE BRETT
1990

BO JACKSON: AN APPRECIATION BY HOWIE LONG

If Bo Jackson and I were both stallions, I think I could command—based on physical characteristics and past performances—a stud fee of, maybe, $500,000.

Bo would get $5 million.

It's like Bo's Secretariat—and I'm Mister Ed.

But Bo's not a horse.

He's an F-16.

In cleats.

Bo does forty yards in 4.2 seconds. He's been timed, legitimately, in 4.18. You can't weigh two hundred and thirty pounds and run that fast. You have to be able to fly.

Bo flies.

I thank the Good Lord I don't have to play defensive back against him. He's the defensive back's worst nightmare. He starts off big and strong and fast, and after ten or fifteen yards, he explodes. He moves into another gear. He's like the five-speed Porsche they won't allow into this country.

When Bo scored his first touchdown for the Los Angeles Raiders, in 1987, a Denver defensive back named Mike Harden tried to stop him by himself. Mike Harden had a better chance of seeing God that day than stopping Bo Jackson.

Bo's running style is unique. His legs are vertical, but from the waist to the shoulders, he's horizontal. When he runs, he's all ass and thighs.

Bo is the future of football.

This is 1990, and he's 2010.

He reminds me of Bobby Orr. Orr was ahead of his time, too.

When I was a kid in Boston, Bobby Orr used to take the puck behind the Bruins' net and look up ice, and the sense of anticipation was unbelievable. In a team sport, every eye was riveted on an individual.

Bobby Orr. Bobby O. B.O. Bo.

Maybe it's a coincidence.

Maybe it isn't.

When Bo gets the ball and looks up field, everyone in the stadium sucks in his breath. You can hear it.

I remember his first game in a Raiders uniform. He didn't play. He sat on the bench. We played Seattle in Los Angeles, and they crushed us. I was on the field for sixty-nine defensive plays, and when I came off, late in the fourth quarter, I was dead. I sat next to Bo.

"I didn't come here to sit on the bench," he said. "If I'm not playing next week, I'm gone."

After three days of practice.

Then he said, "When we go up to Seattle, I'm going to hand these guys their asses."

"Yeah, sure, right, Bo," I said.

I didn't know him yet. I didn't know he only says what he means.

Five weeks later, in Seattle, he made me a spectator for the first time in my career. I was mesmerized. I couldn't wait to see what he'd do next. He scored three touchdowns. He ran for 221 yards. I think *I* saw God that day.

Bo has more ability than anyone I've ever seen. He has greater impact on a crowd than anyone I've ever seen. He is the most awesome physical specimen I've ever seen. I think his mother put Dianabol in his oatmeal.

If Bo ran behind the Los Angeles Rams line that Eric Dickerson ran behind, if Bo played in a John Robinson-style offense that gave him the ball thirty or forty times every game, if Bo put in one full season in the National Football League, I don't think there would be a rushing record standing. He'd gain 200 yards every game. He'd gain 3,000 yards for a season.

It's a shame there aren't enough days in the year for Bo Jackson to realize his potential. It's a shame the seasons have to overlap.

I'm not jealous of Bo's ability, or of the attention he gets, or even of his body. I'm a big dog myself. But I am jealous of him for two reasons. First, he doesn't have to go to training camp, which is vastly overrated, and, second, he doesn't have to spend six months a year at home. He and his wife have the greatest relationship in the world because he's never at home. Two weeks after the football season ends, my wife wants to stab me.

I like Bo. Of course, if you're an ax murderer and you can play outside linebacker and you're wearing the same uniform I am, I like you. But I really like Bo. I'm very comfortable with him. I like to pick on him.

The night before his big game in Seattle, my roommate, Bill Pickel, and I decided to piss Bo off. We called room service and ordered shrimp cocktails, sirloin steak, mashed potatoes, French wine, the works, close to two hundred dollars' worth of dinner, and we signed Bo's name and his room number.

We knew he'd find out when he checked out, but we didn't want to wait that long.

We went down to the lobby and paid one of the women who worked for the hotel ten dollars to call Bo's room and "confirm" the bill.

Bo blew up. He refused to pay. He yelled at the woman.

Then we got a man to call and pretend to be the head of food services. He wanted to know what the problem was. "We've checked it all out, sir," he told Bo. "It's your room number and it's your name on the check. You'll have to pay the bill. Sir."

"Ask the waiter!" Bo screamed. "Ask the waiter who brought up the food if anyone in the room was black! I'm black, you know!"

Bo figured it out. He came to our room, started pounding on our door, calling us names, threatening us.

We ignored him. I'm six-foot-five and two hundred and eighty pounds, and Pickel is bigger. Bo doesn't scare us a bit.

As long as we don't have to tackle him.

—HOWIE LONG
1990

Bo Jackson lay on his stomach on the couch in the living room of his home in the suburbs of Kansas City, his chin resting on his forearms, his muscles straining at a Nike T-shirt, muscles that defy reason. Bo talked, and as he did, tears welled up in the corners of his eyes.

"My mom," he said, "is my dad. She's the only mom *and* dad that I know. Whenever she needs me, I don't care what I'm doing, I'm gonna drop it and go to her, 'cause that's all that matters. That's all that matters now."

A few days earlier, in the spring of 1990, Bo's mom had undergone exploratory surgery at a university hospital in Birmingham, Alabama, and the doctors had found and removed several tumors. Bo and the Kansas City Royals played in Milwaukee that night—teammates could see the tears in his eyes when he took batting practice—and the next morning, sleepless, he got out of bed at 4:30 A.M. and went to the airport and caught a 6:25 A.M. flight to Atlanta and then a connecting flight to Birmingham and went straight to the hospital and to his mother's room.

"I had never seen my mom like that," Bo said. "She was helpless, with tubes in her arms, tubes up her nose, all doped up, and she had lost a lot of weight. She was unconscious, but I could tell she was in a lot of pain. I pulled up a chair and sat there beside her bed and just rubbed her hands. I sat there for a couple of hours, rubbing her hands, looking at her, and the more I looked at her, the more I realized how important your family is, how your family's health and well-being is more important than anything else that's out there."

Bo turned on his back and stared wet-eyed at the ceiling of his living room, thinking. Bo almost always thinks before he speaks. Then he speaks slowly, not painfully slowly, but slowly enough for him to pick his words the way he picks his holes on the football field, looking for the right opening, choosing the right move. He still has traces of the stutter that tormented his childhood, but the stutter does not bother him—he pauses, relaxes, works his way through it—nor does it bother the listener, who after a while begins to realize, with some surprise, exposing misconceived preconceptions, that Bo's words, like Bo himself, have both substance and style. Bo is full of surprises.

"I try to visualize life without my mom," Bo said, "and I just can't. Really. You sit up and that thought crosses your mind and you just want to get it out of your mind altogether. I just lost an aunt and uncle; it hasn't been five months. Lost them four weeks apart. My youngest aunt. My favorite uncle. Aunt Willie Jean and Uncle Jesse."

Bo lifted himself onto an elbow and remembered good times. "When we were little, on Saturdays during the fall," he said, "my Uncle Jesse would pick out a hog and take his little .22 rifle and hit him right between the eyes and drop him right there, and then we would have a family feast. It was one of the few times the men in the family would get together. They'd have their liquor and their beer, and my cousins and I would sit around and watch.

"They had this big cast-iron pot and they'd fill it with water and boil the water and then they'd get a fifty-gallon drum and slide the hog in and get old croaker sacks, burlap sacks, and lay them over one side of the hog and get the hot water and pour it over the croaker sacks and onto the hog's skin. Then they'd give my cousin Jason and me sharp knives and we'd scrape the hair off the hogs, real coarse hair, and once we got the hair off, then they'd hang him up and gut him, and then get the saws out and just cut him up. We had this big saltbox, it had salt on the bottom, and we'd put a layer of meat in there and cover it with salt, another layer of meat and cover it with salt, keep doing that. Then they would take the head, take it up to the house, wash it, clean it out, cook it and make country souse, hogshead cheese.

"Me and my cousin, we'd hang around until they gutted the hog out and then we'd go over and get the hog's liver, wash it out, go up to my cousin's house, get some salt and black pepper, put it on the liver and put it on a stick and go back down to where they were boiling the water and cook the liver over the fire and eat it.

"We would always do stuff like that. Or we would help my Aunt Idelle, Jason's mom, clean the chitterlings, the hog's intestines. It's a gross process." Bo stopped and grinned. "I say it's gross now," he said, "but when we were kids, it was fun. We'd clean the intestines—get the shit out—and throw it on each other."

Bo turned back to the present. The week had been a cruel one, not only for him, but for several of the Royals. Outfielder Jim Eisenreich, who had overcome a nervous disorder called Tourette's syndrome to become a big league ballplayer, had lost his father to cancer. Pitcher Tom Gordon's uncle, the man who had taught him how to pitch, had died the day before Bo's mom was operated on. The mother of Glenn Ezell, the bullpen coach, had also died. All in the same week.

On the field, the Royals were struggling, playing dreadfully, ruining their championship hopes, but their manager, Duke Wathan, gave the grieving Royals time off to be with their families. Wathan understood.

Bo missed four games while he sat by his mother's side in the Birmingham hospital. He did not eat for more than two days, not until an old friend, working in the hospital, practically forced him to go to lunch.

"I really didn't have an appetite," Bo said, "The only thing I was concerned about was trying to get Mom well, to do whatever I could to make her comfortable, to make sure the doctors were giving her the best treatment they could give her."

Bo sat up. He faced a formal portrait—of Bo, his wife Linda and their sons, Garrett and Nicholas—the one personal touch in the living room. Not an athletic trophy in sight, not a single photo of Bo in uniform—football or baseball. Which tells you everything about Bo Jackson's priorities.

"I didn't expect to see my mom like that," Bo said. "It really floored me. She was always so strong and now she was so helpless. I cried. Really cried. Not just little tears. Worst I cried since one of my friends drowned when we were teenagers.

"Finally, my mom came to and opened her eyes and looked at me and said, 'What are *you* doing here?' and I said, 'Well, I just come to see my girl,' and then she went out again for about twenty minutes, and when she opened her eyes again, she caught me wiping tears from my eyes and she said, 'Why are you cryin'?' And I said, ''Cause I just don't want you to be sick. I want you to get well so you can go home.'

"And she went back out and I just sat there and sat there and sat there and I thought about everything she did for me and everything she meant to me."

The doctors came and told Bo that as far as they could see, his mother would recover completely. She would regain her strength.

Bo's mother's name is Florence Jackson Bond. Her eighth child, her fourth of five sons, was born on November 30, 1962, not far from Birmingham, in Bessemer, Alabama, which was then a steel town, the mills still open. Her name then was Florence Jackson. She named the child Vincent Edward Jackson, after her favorite television actor, Vince Edwards, the man who portrayed Dr. Ben Casey.

Now even Florence Bond calls her son Bo.

BO—AS OTHERS SEE HIM

"**I**f you don't change your ways, you're going to be in jail or hell, sure as I'm sitting here."
—FLORENCE JACKSON BOND

"**H**e's got as much talent as Mickey Mantle or Willie Mays."
—DICK EGAN
Major League Scouting Bureau

"**W**hen you're talking about Bo Jackson, you're not talking about a normal person. You're talking about a guy from another planet."
—PAT DYE
Football coach
Auburn University

"**H**e makes his body do what his mind tells it to do. That's as unique as the body he has."
—JACK CROWE
Offensive coordinator
Auburn University

"**H**e's one of the finest backs who has ever played the game."
—JOHNNY MAJORS
Football coach
University of Tennessee

"**B**o is far and away the best young baseball player I've ever seen."
—HAL BAIRD
Baseball coach
Auburn University

"**B**o is the best pure athlete in America."
—KEN GONZALES
Scout
Kansas City Royals

"**H**e's the highest-rated pro football prospect that ever came out."
—DAVE HANNER
Scout
Green Bay Packers

"**P**otentially, I've never seen anybody with the batting strength this kid has."
—DICK HOWSER
Manager
Kansas City Royals

"**I** swear I'm looking at Ted Williams."
—TOMMY JONES
Manager
Memphis Chicks

"**W**hen Bo takes batting practice, there's always the feeling that you're going to see something you never saw before."
—BRET SABERHAGEN
Pitcher
Kansas City Royals

"**B**o is the only baseball player that you sense can do whatever he wants, and you can't wait to see him do it."
—WILLIE WILSON
Outfielder
Kansas City Royals

"**Y**ou get a player like this once in a decade if you're lucky."
—WILL CLARK
First baseman
San Francisco Giants

"Bo Jackson's the best athlete I've ever seen in a baseball uniform."

—SPARKY ANDERSON
Manager
Detroit Tigers

"Very possibly, you're looking at the finest athlete this country has seen in the last fifty years."

—BOOMER ESIASON
Quarterback
Cincinnati Bengals

"He's just too big and too fast for us cornerbacks to bring down. Linebackers, too. I've never seen an athlete like him before."

—MIKE HAYNES
Defensive back
Los Angeles Raiders

"I don't think we'll see a running back of his magnitude, speed, grace, power and excitement for quite some time."

—VINCE EVANS
Quarterback
Los Angeles Raiders

"If he gets by you, you don't chase him, you just stand there and say, 'Wow, look at him run.' I've never seen anything like it."

—BOB GOLIC
Nose tackle
Los Angeles Raiders

"The guy is the greatest back I've ever played against. He's flat-out the best I've seen."

—RANDY DIXON
Defensive back
Cincinnati Bengals

"I've never seen anyone so fast and so strong. When God was handing out talent, Bo got it all."

—LINDEN KING
Linebacker
Los Angeles Raiders

"It's as if the Deity said, 'I want to make an athletic body,' and, *poof*, he made Bo. The guy has a perfect God-given physique."

—TODD CHRISTENSEN
Tight end
Los Angeles Raiders

"Bo looks all muscle—that is, his ears look like they have muscles. His nose looks like it has muscles. When you see him barefoot, even his toes look as if they've got muscles."

—IRA BERKOW
Sports columnist
New York Times

"I don't think I've seen anybody combine power and speed like that since Mickey Mantle."

—TOM LASORDA
Manager
Los Angeles Dodgers

"He's in a league somewhere up in the heavens."

—TONY LA RUSSA
Manager
Oakland A's

"This guy is not only in a league by himself. He's in two leagues by himself."

—MIKE DOWNEY
Sports columnist
Los Angeles Times

"You're my new idol."

—KIRBY PUCKETT
Outfielder
Minnesota Twins

"He's such an incredible baseball talent. God, I don't know why he even considers football."

—JIM LEFEBVRE
Manager
Seattle Mariners

"If he devoted himself to football, there's no doubt in my mind that he'd be the greatest ever to play the game."

—TIM GOAD
Nose tackle
New England Patriots

"In at least two ways, I think Bo and I are [alike]. If I put my mind to it, I've always believed I could do anything I want, and I've heard him say the same thing. The other similarity is that neither of us is very easily amazed [by what we do]. You have to expect things of yourself before you can do them."

—MICHAEL JORDAN

1

I COULDN'T STEAL A FATHER

I'm not going to tell you everything about myself. I'm going to hold a little back. Just a few things I've never told anybody. You understand. It gets harder and harder for me to find a little piece of myself I can keep for myself. All I want is a little piece. I'll give you the rest.

Remember "The Brady Bunch" from television? They were the perfect family. Everybody loved them. I hated them. I hated them because they had a mother *and* a father and enough food on the table for all of them.

We never had enough food. But at least I could beat on other kids and steal their lunch money and buy myself something to eat. I could steal candy bars, too. But I couldn't steal a father. I couldn't steal a father's hug when I needed one. I couldn't steal a father's ass-whipping when I needed one. I didn't have a man to look up to, or to listen to.

Biologically, I did have a father, of course. His name was—and is—A. D. Adams, and he used to work in the steel mills, like most of the men in Bessemer. He was my father and the father of two of my sisters. He was married, but not to my mother. He had his own family on the other side of town. He'd come by sometimes and give me a little money, but then I wouldn't see him again for months.

I lived with my mother and my brothers and sisters in a three-room house on a dirt road on the outskirts of town, in a rural neighborhood called Raimond. When I was born, we had all eight children living in the house. After my sister Millicent was born, we had nine living at home. That was the most. My oldest sister, Jennifer, moved to Chicago before my baby brother, Clarence, was born.

Nobody had a bed all for himself. We had two beds in the bedroom, and usually we'd sleep two to a bed, one at the top and one at the bottom. The rest of us would sleep on the floor. In the winter, we had a coal stove for the bedroom and a gas heater for the living room, and most of the time I tried to sleep right in front of the heater. Sometimes I'd wake up with burn marks on my butt where I bumped against the heater during the night.

The gas heater would warm the kitchen, too. There was no door between the living room and the kitchen, where my mom slept.

We didn't have indoor plumbing. Nobody did out in the country where we lived. We had an outhouse. When we got a new outhouse, we thought that was heaven. Kids came to see it: tarpaper roof, concrete floor, painted green, the same as our house.

Sometimes we didn't have anything to eat but grits and margarine. Sometimes we didn't have anything at all. I'd be home and not have anything to eat and then I'd go over to a friend's house and they'd have a nice dinner on the table, and they'd ask me do I want anything, and I had so much pride I'd say no, and my stomach would be singing a tune.

When I asked my mom why we didn't have a refrigerator full of food, why my Aunt Bea used to have to bring us leftovers from the school where she was a janitor, my mom used to say, "Well, I provide for all of you the best that I can, and you have to accept what you got, and be thankful for it."

I knew how hard my mom worked, but I wasn't thankful. I was angry. I was a hoodlum and a bully. I was the bad little Jackson kid—and foolish enough to be proud of it. When I watched "Sesame Street," my favorite character was Oscar, the grouch who lived in the garbage can.

I fired rocks through the windows of passing cars and I ran when they swerved off the road. I threw rocks at the heads of other kids, too—and I had a strong arm and good aim. I once beat on one of my cousins with a softball bat—one of my *girl* cousins. Twice I raised a loaded gun and aimed it at kids who had crossed me, and twice I came close to squeezing the trigger, to shooting them and probably destroying me.

My mom used to whip me with a cherry switch and warn me I was going to end up in the penitentiary, but I didn't mind the switch and I didn't hear the words. I knew I didn't have a father to answer to.

I used to take money from my mom. Most of the time, I just took pocket change, but once, when I was five years old, I found a gold envelope with a big word on it: INSURANCE. I opened it up and saw a bunch of bills and took it and went next door, to an old gutted-out house, and hid the envelope there. A few days later, I was playing with some of my friends, and I started bragging, "I got some money," and we went and got it—I think they gypped me out of most of it—and we walked about five miles to Burger King and stuffed ourselves. I don't know how my mom got the money to make her insurance payment, but she did.

She used to leave her purse lying on the floor next to her bed in the kitchen. Early in the morning, I'd crawl in, open her purse, grab a quarter or fifty cents, then crawl back to the living room and go to sleep. One morning, about six o'clock, she caught me. She just flipped over and said, "Don't you move. You keep your hands right there."

She lay back down till about seven-thirty and then she got up and tied me to the bedpost and wore my ass out. She whipped me good. She used the extension cord. When she was really angry, she used the extension cord instead of the cherry switch. The extension cord didn't break. It gave you welts that looked like somebody played tic-tac-toe on your back.

Some of my friends and I had a passion for stealing bicycles. We called ourselves The Bicycle Bandits. I could steal a bike, take it home and, within an hour and a half, strip the bike, throw it in a fire, burn the paint off, spray-paint it a different color and then ride it down the street, doing wheelies past the house I stole it from. I only got caught one time, and a couple of kids saw me get caught and laughed at me. I kicked their asses.

Kids wanted to be my friends just so I wouldn't beat them up. I was hard on everybody who wasn't my friend. Keith Mack was my best friend. I was envious of him—and not just because he had a father. His father was a scoutmaster, and Keith and his brothers were the first kids in our neighborhood to have footballs and bikes and then go-carts and motorbikes.

I wanted to live the way the Macks did, and if I had, I probably never would have gotten out of Bessemer. I'd probably still be there, like Keith is. But I *had to* get out; he didn't.

I stuttered from the time I started talking. That was one thing my father did give me. He stuttered, too. I stuttered so bad by the time I was in the first grade at the Raimond Elementary School, my mom told the teacher to keep me back, and she did.

That pissed me off. I was one of the smartest kids in my class—I could *write* my name, not just print it, before anyone else could—but because of my stuttering, I couldn't keep up with the "normal" kids. I knew I could read better than them, but when I'd go to read out loud in school, I'd get stuck on a word, and some of the kids would start laughing at me. I never forgot which ones laughed. If you laughed at me when I stuttered in class, I'd beat the shit out of you when we got out of school. I did that religiously from the first grade through the sixth.

I was older than almost all the kids in my class, and bigger than them, and stronger. I used to let my older brothers and my cousins punch me in the chest as hard as they wanted, even the ones who were six and seven years older than me, and I wouldn't cry. I wouldn't flinch. I was tough as a wild boar. They called me Bo'-hog, which is a Southern term for a wild boar, and then they shortened it to Bo. They also called me the Little Nappy-haired Rock Chunker, which they shortened to Nap.

I discovered sex when I was seven years old. Sort of. We used to see the grown-ups doing it. We used to sneak around the house and peek through the neighbors' windows and then we would mimic the grown-ups. We called it doing the grown-up, or doing the nasty. We didn't really know what we were supposed to be doing, but we knew it went somewhere down there. We used to get a big old box that had come with a refrigerator in it or a stove and we'd climb inside and say we were playing house. That was my favorite game, back then.

I liked playing hide-and-go-get-it, too. It was just like hide-and-go-seek, except the boys would cover their eyes and count to a hundred by fives, and the girls would hide, and then we'd go look for them, and you could hunch up against the one you found, rub up against her, clothes on clothes. I always found the prettiest girl first. It wasn't just luck. I peeked.

I hated school then. I didn't want to learn anything. I didn't want to listen to anybody. I used to have to wear my older sister's shoes to school sometimes because I didn't have any of my own. One of the kids made fun of my shoes—once. He remembered seeing my sister wear them, and he knew they were girls' shoes, and he made a wisecrack. I whacked him in the head after school.

Beating up on kids was the only thing I really enjoyed in elementary school. Especially kids older than me, two or three grades older. "Give me your lunch money," I'd tell them, and if they started to cry and say they wouldn't be able to have anything to eat, I'd say, "Okay, I'll lend you back your fifty cents. But you got to bring me seventy-five cents tomorrow, understand?"

I didn't even know what interest was, but I was charging it.

They understood, and they paid—or they got their butts whipped. I had a regular business going. I even hired kids to beat up other kids for me. I didn't have time to beat up all of them myself.

I intimidated everybody at the Raimond school. One day I got into it with a kid named Michael. "I'll get you after school," I promised him. I knew he went home one way and I went home the other way, so I had to get him in the front yard of the school.

That day, Mr. Hobson, the principal, walked us out. As soon as Mr. Hobson went back inside, I was going to wear Michael's butt out. But Michael turned to the principal and said, "Mr. Hobson, Mr. Hobson, will you tell Vincent not to bother me? He said he was going to beat me up."

Mr. Hobson looked at me and said, "Boo"—I had a hundred nicknames—"Boo, what are you bothering him for?"

"I'm gonna get him," I said. I didn't care who knew.

"Oh no you're not," Mr. Hobson said. "You come back in school with me."

He kept me in school until everyone else was gone. I had to walk home alone, a mile and a half, most of it through the woods. My house was on one side of the woods, in a black neighborhood, and the school was on the other, in a white neighborhood. I started walking toward the woods, and some high school kids came driving down the road in a blue Mustang. I'll never forget it.

I guess they saw me and aimed the car at me and

got to within ten yards of me and then skidded and stopped and jumped out and started yelling at me. "Come here, nigger!" they hollered. "We're gonna kick your ass!"

For no reason, no reason at all. I didn't even know these guys. "We're gonna getcha, nigger," they said. "We're gonna getcha."

I took off. I raced into the woods, and they chased me. I ran them all around the woods, wore them out. They chased me toward a deep ditch, had to be ten or twelve feet wide, maybe more, and I leaped over the ditch and ran up a hill toward the start of my neighborhood, the black neighborhood, and when I got to the top of the hill I looked around and they were down in the ditch—they couldn't jump it—and I turned and started throwing rocks at them like you never saw rocks thrown. I don't know whether I hit them or not. I didn't stop to look. I just kept throwing.

That was the first time I really experienced prejudice, the only time I ever really felt threatened by it, threatened physically. I learned something. I made it a point from then on not to be kept after school. It was too dangerous.

My cousins and I, we lived for the weekends. Friday nights, my Aunt Bea would turn her house into sort of a social club. She'd start cooking around two in the afternoon. People would get paid on Friday and they would get off work and they wouldn't even go home to change. They'd go right to my aunt's house and buy themselves some chicken or a fish sandwich and a beer.

I tried a beer once when I was a kid. It was the awfulest-tasting thing I ever put in my mouth. I took one sip and poured the rest down the sink. I still can't drink more than one beer or maybe a couple of glasses of wine. Forget about hard liquor. When I was only five or six, I found a bottle of white lightning in the woods, moonshine liquor, and I drank almost the whole bottle before I passed out. My brothers and sisters had to carry me home and hide me from my mom for two days before I could stand up alone. I tried cigarettes, too, took one puff and my head got light and I had to lie down. I was ripped. I still don't smoke. And I tried pot once, found a marijuana cigarette in a plastic bag and smoked it and then ate everything in the refrigerator and got dizzy and sick and never tried it again—never will.

At my Aunt Bea's parties, the men would play cards all night long, and I'd run sandwiches and beers for them and put the money in my aunt's little box. I'd go under the card table and if anyone dropped some money, I'd steal it. I'd get maybe five or ten dollars a night and put it in my pocket and then go out and buy two-for-a-penny cookies and twelve-ounce soft drinks for twelve cents and a bag of potato chips for a dime. I ate all kinds of junk. Maybe that's why I'm having bridges put in on both sides of my mouth now.

I'd sleep Friday nights at my Aunt Bea's house with my cousins, and then Saturday morning, she'd cook us a big breakfast: fried chicken, rice, biscuits, gravy.

Sunday was the best day. My cousins and me, Jason and his brother Lodge, we'd get up early, our moms would make us go to church and then we'd hurry home and change our clothes and get on our bikes and go. We would always go east, toward the horizon. We thought that was where the world ended. We thought once you got to the other side of the trees, you were in outer space. We would ride and ride and ride, but we never got to the other side of the trees.

We jammed everything we could into the day, because we didn't want it to end; we didn't want Monday to come and we'd have to go back to school. We had crab-apple fights—everyone wanted to be on my side because they knew how I could throw—and when it was warm, we would stop and go swimming, in our water hole or in the lake that was on the property of the local dairy. The water in the water hole was always red—real red, clay red. The water in the lake was clearer, but the man who owned the dairy put up a barbed-wire fence and told us, "If I catch you swimming in that lake, I'm gonna whip your ass."

Naturally, we swam there anyway. We used to have to walk through the woods and then go through some blackberry bushes and climb through the barbed wire to get down to the water. One day we ate a bunch of blackberries and then, instead of leaving our clothes in the woods the way we usually did, we left them up on the bank and jumped in the lake.

One of the men who worked for the dairy happened to be riding his horse up on a hill overlooking the lake, and he spotted us and rode around the back way and came up behind us, right by the dam where our clothes were, and fired his rifle up in the air. We jumped out of the water, took off without a stitch of clothes on, picked our way through the barbed wire very carefully and dashed into the woods. The man on the horse found our clothes and threw them in the lake, right by the drain.

We ran three or four hundred yards through the woods, then slowed down and walked to the sanitation dump, which was about a mile away, to see if we could find some clothes. We couldn't find anything, so we decided to go to my cousin's house, which was the closest place we could go. To get there, we only had to go past one house. An old lady was sitting out on the porch. We had to go past her, buck-ass naked.

"Don't say nothing," my cousin said. "She'll think we're from Florida."

We didn't know where Florida was. All we knew was that it was supposed to be so hot in Florida that people walked around naked.

I loved to go swimming. One summer I was supposed to go to Chicago—to stay with my oldest sister, Jennifer—and the day I was going to leave, my mom warned me not to go swimming. "Don't you go across the mountain to that swimming hole," she said. "You go swimming, you're not going to Chicago." That was all I needed, somebody telling me I couldn't do something.

I took off with my buddies across the mountain, went for a swim, got back early and started packing to go with my baby sister to Chicago. "You aren't going nowhere," my mom said, "'cause I told you don't go swimming. I told you not to go around that mountain and swim in that water hole." Mom put my baby sister on the plane and I stayed home all summer. I never did step out of Alabama till I was eighteen and never got on an airplane till I was nineteen.

Summers in Bessemer, we hung around the rec center. We'd do artwork, make things out of plaster, drink Pepsis and shoot pool and play Ping-Pong. One day I was getting ready to take on the winner of the last Ping-Pong game, and my cousin came out of the rec center and saw me standing with the paddle and she thought I had just lost, so she yanked the paddle out of my hand and, as she did, she dug her fingernails into my hand and scratched me up. I grabbed the paddle back from her and she yanked it back and then I pushed her and she hit me with the paddle.

She was about fourteen, and I was about twelve. I turned around and went out to the baseball field and grabbed a softball bat and came back and swung it at her. The first time, I swung so hard I missed her and fell down. I jumped up and swung again and missed her again. But the third time, I connected. I hit her as hard as I could, right in the kidneys, brought her to her knees. She went down on the ground, and I stood over her, fixing to hit her across the back with the bat, and one of my older sisters—she was working at the rec center—grabbed me and stopped me. I had so much anger. I took it out on everybody.

Just a couple of weeks later, I was at the rec center, playing pool, and a guy who was two or three years older than me took my turn, just pushed me out of the way. I pushed him back, and he shoved me out the door. "You be here when I get back," I yelled, and I went home and got my mother's shotgun. I ran out the back door with one of my sisters shouting at me, "You better come back here, 'cause I'm gonna tell."

I went to the rec center and the guy had left. He was on his way home, cutting through the woods. I ran after him and caught sight of him just as he was about to come out of the woods and go into his yard. I was no more than maybe forty yards away, and I raised the shotgun, fixing to shoot, and I would've blown him away if he hadn't stepped behind a tree. I lowered the gun.

Then he went into his house, and I went home and found out my sister had locked me out—with the gun. "You aren't getting inside until Momma comes," she said.

I had to sit outside with the shotgun for about three hours, and while I was sitting there, a blackbird flew by, and I took aim at him and—*boom!*—nothing came down but feathers and a beak. I blew him away. My mom used the extension cord that night. She told me I was going to end up in reform school. She was going to send me there, just like she sent one of my older brothers there. He told me what it was like. He didn't sleep the first three nights, fighting off guys who were trying to rape him.

I was just going into the sixth grade then. Nobody ever beat me up in elementary school, nobody except my older brothers and sisters, and that didn't count because their name was Jackson, too. The only time I ever got beat up by anybody else was when I was in the seventh grade and I jumped on a ninth grader who was about a foot taller than me and about thirty pounds heavier. He smacked me in the nose twice and knocked me out.

When I came to, I had to get even. I knew he took the same school bus that I took, and got off at the same stop—right in front of my house. I knew he had to walk a couple of hundred yards from the bus stop to his house. There was a field between my house and the road he had to take. I ran home from the bus stop, grabbed my brother's .22 rifle and went out in the field to get him.

When he started down the road to his house, I raised the .22 and got him square in my sights. I could have filled him so full of lead they would've had to pick him up with a magnet.

Then I started thinking. "If I shoot him," I said to myself, "I could go to jail, or I could go to reform school, and then I'd be up all night, fighting to keep the guys from raping me." That scared the hell out of me.

So I shot a tree instead. He heard the shot and turned and saw me, dropped his books and hauled his ass home. He ran like a scared jackrabbit, and I kept shooting behind him, not even close, and he hit his front porch and didn't even open the screen door, he just went right through it, right through the damn screen door.

He moved away from Bessemer before I could get even with him. But I owe him. If I ever run across him, anywhere, his ass is mine.

Let me tell you one more story about the days when I couldn't hold the anger down, when I wanted to lash out at everyone. It happened during the summer of 1976, when I was thirteen, almost fourteen, getting ready to enter junior high.

My buddies and I still hung around the rec center almost every day in the summer, long enough to shoot some pool and eat the free lunch. Then, when we got bored, we'd go across the mountain to the swimming hole with the red, red water. On the way to the swimming hole, we'd pass a place that was owned by a minister. He had a pigpen filled with big old hogs. We'd stop off and beat on the pigs, throw rocks at them and hit them with sticks till they died. We killed a bunch of them. It was something to do.

Once we went three days in a row and each day we beat on one hog that must have weighed four hundred, five hundred pounds, and he just wouldn't die. Finally, on the fourth day, we got him down, he was whipped, and we all gathered around him, maybe fifteen or twenty of us, beating him with our sticks. All of a sudden, we heard someone cry out, "Hey! Get out of here!"

It was a man who was doing some work for the minister. I didn't even look at him close. I just dropped my stick and ran. We all ran.

I jumped the fence that went around the pigpen and sprinted about fifteen or twenty yards, heading right for a ditch that had to be eighteen or twenty feet wide. I hit the edge full speed and took off and, as I sailed over the ditch, hoping I'd reach the other side, I looked down and saw a ditch full of dead pigs. We always wondered what the minister did with the pigs we beat to death. I cleared the ditch—just barely.

It was about a mile and a half from the pigpen to my house, and I ran all the way, through the woods, made it home, took off my clothes with the pig's blood all over them, put on fresh clothes, washed the mud off my shoes and was sitting in my living room when the man who was working for the minister pulled up in his car and knocked on our front door. My mom answered the door. The man told her he saw me killing the minister's pigs.

"Not me," I said. "Not me. I wasn't there."

The man stepped into our house. "I know you were there," the man said. "I cut your hair every other week. I know you. That was you."

The man was my barber. He didn't believe me. My mom didn't believe me, either.

"They killed two, three thousand dollars' worth of pigs," the man said.

"If the man who owns the pigs wants to send his ass to reform school," my mom said, "then send him, 'cause I'm tired of his ways. I can't do nothin' with him." She looked at me and said, "You're going, boy."

"Who else was with you?" the man said.

"I wasn't with nobody," I lied. "I was here."

"I'll tell you what," the man said. "If you don't tell me who was with you, you are going to reform school—you and only you."

I ratted. Only time in my life. I ratted on everybody. No way I was going to reform school. No way I was going to get raped.

I gave him every name, and we all got grounded, every single one of us. We had to stay at home, doing chores, except when we got odd jobs, mowing lawns mostly, giving everything we earned to the minister till we paid him off for the pigs we killed.

When we went back to school in the fall, to junior high, everybody had heard about what we did. They called us The Pig Killers.

I got my last whipping when I was in junior high. I was big then, and my mom stood over me with the extension cord in her right hand and a .38 in her left, and she said, "You run, or you try to take this extension cord away from me, and I'm gonna bust you in the ass with this pistol." I stood there and took my beating, and maybe I finally woke up, finally realized that my mom was right, that the way I was going, I was just looking for trouble, heading straight to reform school or to prison.

I was scared. That's why I started to change. That was the first step. Nothing else. Just fear. The next step was that I began thinking if I didn't want to go to prison, where did I want to go?

I wanted to go to college. I wanted to be an engineer. An electrical engineer. Or maybe a pilot. I loved airplanes. I loved watching them climb up in the sky and disappear beyond the horizon. I wondered where they went.

I began thinking that maybe there was a world beyond the horizon, and I found out pretty soon that playing ball was going to help me get there.

They lay in bed with their arms around each other, Bo Jackson and Nicholas Jackson, not yet two years old, the younger of Bo's two sons, Bo in miniature. Garrett (Spud) Jackson, Nick's three-year-old big brother, was off at his Montessori nursery school, and Linda, Bo's wife, seven months pregnant, was at the obstetrician's, undergoing an ultrasound scan, the test to gauge the baby's size, due date and gender. Bo was baby-sitting, which may be his best sport.

Bo sat up and flicked the remote-control switch, changing the television to a program about hunting and fishing, his other passions. As Bo lay back in the bed, Nick curled his little arm under his dad's sequoia neck, and Bo turned and kissed Nick's cheek, then buried his nose in Nick's neck, father and son, massive and miniature, intertwined.

Bo heard the sound of a door opening. "Girl!" he called out. "You better come in here!"

Linda Jackson poked her head into the bedroom. She met Bo through a mutual friend when he was a junior at Auburn, and she was a graduate student. They liked each other, became friends and studied together, elbow-to-elbow at the kitchen table in Linda's apartment, neither suspecting that their relationship would graduate to more than friendship.

She is now on the brink of her Ph.D. in counseling psychology; she is completing her thesis, a study of women who were sexually abused as children and the impact of that abuse upon their roles as mothers. Linda is a bright woman, the independent daughter of an independent woman who, widowed young, worked for an insurance company in a small Alabama town and worked hard enough to send two sons and a daughter through college. Linda is as sturdy in her way as Bo is in his.

"I know, Vincent," Linda said, teasing. "I know."

"Tell me," Bo demanded. "Or do you want me to call the doctor?"

Linda laughed. "Doctor says we can now tell the world Miss Morgan is coming," she said.

"Morgan?" Bo said. "Morgan? It's a girl?"

"Definitely," Linda said. "Definitely a girl. He said you can go buy pink stuff, 'cause this is surely a girl. We had three opinions in there and . . ."

"Morgan Vincentia," Bo said, beaming. "Morgan Vincentia Jackson."

". . . and all three of them said it's a girl!"

Linda looked at her husband. He wore only briefs, clinging to his thirty-five-inch waist, his forty-eight-inch chest bare. "Between you and Garrett and Nicholas," Linda said, "Morgan will never have a husband. I don't think anybody will come see her. You'll scare them all away."

Bo faked a mean scowl. "I told you don't come home if it isn't a girl," he said.

Linda handed Bo the X-ray pictures the doctors had

taken, and Bo stared at the curled-up child who was not yet born. He had not seen Spud, his first child, until six weeks *after* he was born. Bo wanted to see him sooner, but he was playing baseball when Spud was born, and he and Linda were not yet married.

The first chance he got, the first break in his baseball schedule after Spud was born, Bo went to Auburn, straight to Linda's apartment. He arrived just as the baby was awakening from a nap. Spud opened his eyes, looked up at his father for the first time—and smiled. Bo picked him up, hugged him and, for an hour, walked around the apartment, holding Spud, caressing him. Then Bo lay down on a couch, pressed the baby against his chest and they both fell asleep. When they awoke, Bo changed Spud and fed him and he was hooked. Four months later, Bo proposed to Spud's mother.

Now Linda kissed Bo and led Nicholas out of the bedroom and into his favorite room, the kitchen. Nick eats all day long. He can eat anything he wants, Bo says, except junk food. Bo does not want to visit the sins of the father upon his sons.

Bo began getting dressed, slipping into sport shirt and slacks, in shades of tan and brown. "We're going to move Nick out of his room now and put him in with Spud," Bo said. "Just move his ass out, ship him out. We'll put Spud in the top bunk and Nick in the bottom. I got to put rails up on both beds. Might as well get started redecorating now, 'cause the baby's going to be here in two months."

The thought delighted him. "She'll probably be a real tomboy up until about eight, nine, ten years old," he said, "because the only kids she'll have to play with are her two brothers, and they'll be riding bicycles and go-carts, and motorbikes, and she'll want to do it, too."

Bo couldn't stop grinning. "I always told my wife when we have a girl, it's going to be our last kid," he said. "We're not going to have no more kids. I'm shutting down the factory."

———

Bo could glimpse the future—for his children, for himself. "I got this year with the Raiders and next year and then who knows?" Bo said. "If they want to pay me a shitload of money for a few more years, I'd be crazy to turn them down. By the time the kids are ready to go to college, I'm going to need all the money I can get. I don't want them going to Florida State. I sure as hell don't want them going to Alabama. I don't even want them going to Auburn. I want them to go to Vanderbilt or Duke. I want them to go to a place where I know they'll get a good education, Georgia Tech, or maybe Virginia."

Bo nodded his head. "They're going to have all the latest technology in terms of learning. They're going to have computers in their rooms, and we're going to make certain they do their lessons. I think they're probably getting their smarts from their mom. I hope so. Spud already knows twice as much as he's supposed to, and Nick is following in his footsteps."

Bo hesitated. "My ultimate goal," he said, "is to have my kids go to Harvard or Yale."

That could be the best thing ever to happen to Ivy League football.

"They would probably be the most boringest kids right after they graduate from Harvard or Yale," said the most giftedest athlete, "but they'll be guaranteed a good job after they get out of there."

And then the Auburn man went into his kitchen and kissed his wife and son goodbye and went off to his job at Royals Stadium, a part-time job that pays him a million dollars a year. It's a good job.

2 | I COULDN'T PLAY BASKETBALL— OR DANCE

When I was little, I never dreamed about being O. J. Simpson. I never dreamed about being Reggie Jackson. I never dreamed about being them because, when I was little, I knew their names, but I didn't really know who they were. I didn't watch sports on television. I was too busy playing, playing everything. I cross-trained, even then.

My grandfather, on my mother's side, was an athlete. George (Snag) Jackson. They called him Snag because he was a catcher and he caught bare-handed and he could just reach out and snag a hardball. My mother played ball, too. Softball. She was pretty good, too—or so she tells me. My father wasn't a ballplayer, as far as I know. But maybe I get my size from him.

They call him Big Track. He's about twice as big as I am.

I guess my first game was stickball, playing in the street, using a branch off a tree or a sawed-off handle from an old broom, hitting a rubber ball or a beat-up old tennis ball. I hit some long home runs in stickball, over the woods and into the front yard of the bootlegger who lived down the street from us.

I played stickball with my friends and my cousins—I had a million of them in the neighborhood—and with my older brothers, Jerry and Ronald and Anthony. My brothers were five to ten years older than me, but I always felt I had to compete at their level. I had to throw the ball as hard, hit the ball as far. I did, too, and they weren't bad ballplayers. My brother Jerry—he's five years older than me—played baseball at Lawson Junior College in Birmingham.

My first organized sport was track. I was in the third grade, and one day I was sitting in the back of the class at a corner desk, being punished for being bad, and I looked out the window and saw the track team practicing. They had a rule—only fourth, fifth and sixth graders on the team, no third graders—but I didn't know that. I snuck out and started practicing and outran everybody, and Mr. Hobson, who was the track coach at Raimond as well as the principal, said I could be on the team. I won two races the first meet I entered. I loved track and field, loved running and jumping. That was my favorite sport right up into college.

I started playing Little League baseball that summer. Nobody else wanted to be a catcher, so I said, "I'll catch." I liked catching. You got to touch the ball almost every pitch. You got to dive at balls, block them, throw out runners. I could throw them out from my knees; I didn't even have to straighten up. I was only ten years old, but I could throw hard without taking a step.

They only let me play in the Little League for a few weeks. Then they said I was too rough for the other kids—most of them were a year or two older than me—and they moved me up to the Pony League, to play against thirteen- and fourteen-year-olds. I caught and pitched in the Pony League. I was a pretty good pitcher. I struck out most of the batters I faced. My best pitch was my curve, and we called it the rope-a-dope, after Muhammad Ali.

For the last out of the game, when I was pitching, everybody on my team would take off their gloves and sit down, and it would just be me and the catcher and the batter. I'd blow two fastballs by him, and then my teammates would start yelling, "Give him the rope-a-dope! Give him the rope-a-dope!" I'd drop down and throw the curve, and the batter would almost always swing and miss, and we'd walk off the field.

By the time I was a teenager, I was playing in the industrial league, mostly against grown men. Scouts used to come around to watch, looking for the new Willie Mays or Hank Aaron or Willie McCovey, who were all from Alabama. The scouts didn't believe I was just thirteen or fourteen.

When we were in the ninth grade, one of my friends, Leroy Mason, made the varsity football team. He was the first ninth grader ever to play for the varsity at McAdory High, which was in a little town called McCalla, right near Bessemer.

Leroy's big brother was a senior and a starting running back for McAdory. He'd bust through the line and go eighty yards for a touchdown, and then Leroy would go in for him and he'd bust through the line and go eighty yards for a touchdown. I played for the junior high team. I wasn't good enough to play for the varsity.

I also wrestled for the junior high. I was a heavyweight. I weighed about a hundred and seventy pounds, and I had to practice against high school juniors and seniors because there was no one my size in the junior high except my coach and he didn't want to mess with me.

My mom didn't want me to wrestle. She'd only seen the sport on television, and she thought we wrestled the same way: jumping off the top rope, sticking fingers in each other's eyes, whacking heads together. "I don't want you doing that," she said, and, as usual, I didn't listen to her.

I was undefeated until, in one match, my opponent and I were grappling for position and—I couldn't believe it—he *pinched* me. I just picked him up and body-slammed him against the mat, I was so mad. The referee stepped in. "Don't do that again," he warned *me*, "or you'll be disqualified." He didn't say anything about pinching.

We got back on the mat and, the next thing I knew, the guy pinched me again. This time I picked him up and slammed his head against the mat and I didn't even wait to be disqualified; I just walked right out of the gym, and that was the end of my wrestling career. My mom was happy. She was afraid I was going to get hurt.

I did make the McAdory varsity track and field team while I was still in junior high. Dick Atchison was my track coach. He later became my football coach and my guidance counselor, and he was as close as I came to having a father. I couldn't have become the human being I am without him. He cared about me. He taught me how to control my temper—at least some of the time.

I used to just wake up with a mean streak in me some days. I could feel it: If *anybody* said *anything* to me, I'd just beat the shit out of him. Coach Atchison taught me to turn that meanness around, to wait until after school and take that meanness out on running the hurdles or high jumping.

I'd learned how to jump at home, practicing on the fence in front of my house. When I was still in elementary school, we had moved out of our three-room house and into a house seven or eight streets away, the house my mom still lives in. She had to take out a loan from the bank to get us the new house. It had indoor plumbing—*two* bathrooms—and if you counted both bathrooms and maybe the hallways, too, it had twelve rooms. They weren't very big rooms—the whole place looks pretty small to me now—but it looked like a palace then. People thought we were rich. I couldn't understand how we could live in such a big house and still not have enough food in the refrigerator.

We had a fence around our house, and my mom always kept the front gate locked so that kids wouldn't cut through our front yard and so that my brothers and sisters and I had to go out the back gate, which was by our driveway. My mom's room was also in the back. She could see who was coming and who was going the back way. But I liked to go out the front and go right up to the fence, which must've been close to five feet high, and jump over it, flat-footed. I'd be off to the playground before my mom knew I was gone.

My mom hated me jumping over the fence in front. "One of these days that damn fence is gonna catch you in the seat of your pants and cut your ass up," she'd yell at me, " and I ain't gonna take you to the doctor, 'cause you got to learn to use the back gate." My mom always could think of more ways I was going to get hurt.

I ended up on the track team because one day, as I was coming off the baseball field, I happened to walk past the high-jump pit. The varsity high jumper was practicing, and he wasn't able to clear six feet, but he was working his way up to it. He had the bar set at five feet, six inches. I stopped and, in my baseball uniform, took a couple of steps and jumped over the bar. Coach Atchison saw my jump and asked me if I'd like to be on the track team.

He taught me the flop, the technique of sliding over the high-jump bar backward. He taught me how to run the hurdles. He made me practice by hurdling folding chairs. He taught me *form* to go along with my speed and my spring. He told me I ought to try the decathlon.

I didn't even know what the decathlon was. But I found out: ten events combined, running, jumping and throwing. Right from the start, I could sprint and hurdle and jump, but I wasn't comfortable with some of the other events. I had no idea how to throw the discus. I threw it flat-footed, just muscled it out, because when I tried to spin and let it fly, the way you're supposed to, I never knew which way it was going. And I couldn't practice the pole vault, because we didn't have a pole at McAdory. I had to borrow one at meets.

I tried not to practice the one-mile run. I never saw any sense in running that far. It was boring.

When I was in the ninth grade, only a few weeks after I found out what the decathlon was, I competed in the state championships, against kids from three hundred high schools. I finished tenth, and I felt great—until I got home. Then I found out that John Robinson had drowned.

John was a good friend. He was one of The Bicycle Bandits when we were young. We loved doing wheelies on the bikes we stole. It didn't make any difference if it was a little bike or a ten-speed, we'd do wheelies. Then we moved up to motorcycles. Most of the guys did. My mom wouldn't let me have a motorcycle. She was afraid I was going to get hurt.

One day John was out riding his motorcycle, and either he ran a red light, or a bus did, and they collided. John broke nearly every bone in his body. They packed him in ice for two weeks and kept him in the hospital for four months, and when he came out, he was a changed person. He didn't even look the same. His hair wasn't nappy any more; it had turned slick, real slick.

The day I competed in the state decathlon, John went fishing with a friend of ours named Red Johnson. They were in a rowboat, and neither of them was wearing a life jacket. Some guys came around the bend in a bass boat, moving fast, and the wake from the bass boat turned over the little boat John and Red were in. Neither of them knew how to swim.

The guys in the bass boat saw John and Red struggling, and they circled back and saved Red, but they couldn't save John. The coroner said later that John panicked and had a heart attack before he drowned.

I cried that night. John was the first person I knew who died so young. He was my own age. I felt so bad for his mom. John's older brother had drowned, too.

The next fall, I was in the tenth grade, and I moved up to the varsity football team. It was no big deal. I didn't care that much about football. I did it mostly to pass the time after baseball season. I suppose you could say football was my hobby, even then.

Leroy Mason and Keith Mack and I became the starting running backs for McAdory, three tenth graders, and for the next three years we shared the ball-carrying. Keith would run a play and then Leroy would run a play and then I'd run a play. I think Leroy was the toughest of the three of us. Keith was the smallest, but he was quick as a cat. I was the biggest.

Leroy and Keith were just as good as I was, but both of them ended up going to junior college in Alabama and never going on to a four-year school. Why'd I make it and they didn't? It all came down to having a father at home. They had better lives at home than I did. It was as simple as that.

Of course my mom didn't want me to play football. She saw the pros play on television, saw how hard they hit, and she figured we did, too. Coach Atchison usually drove me home after practice—he never stopped in front of my house, he just slowed down and I jumped out—and my mom would say, "You like the damn coach so much, you go home with him. Don't you come here!"

She locked me out of the house sometimes, and I'd go to Keith's house—he lived two houses down from me—or I'd sleep in my older sister's car, a broken-down Buick Riviera that wouldn't run any more. That was my bedroom, and later, after my brother Jerry and I fixed it up and put an engine in, it became my first car. A 1967 Riviera. It was just five years younger than me.

My brothers advised me to listen to Mom, to give up football and concentrate on baseball. They weren't worried about me playing two sports; they were worried about me not having a place to sleep. They meant well, just like the people who tell me to give up one sport now, but I didn't pay any attention to them, either.

I did make one concession. I didn't go out for basketball—even though the coaches begged me to. The truth is, I wasn't any good. I was the only black kid in Alabama who couldn't play basketball. I fouled. I couldn't dribble. Kids used to laugh at me. I had a tendency to tuck the ball under my arm and run with it. But I *could* dunk. I used to take a volleyball and start at the foul line and take one big step and dunk. I think I could've been as good as Michael Jordan—if only I could've dribbled and shot and passed.

(I also couldn't dance. At least, I *didn't* dance. I do now. I dance at home with Spud and Nick. I'm not very good, but I will be in a few years, now that I've got Morgan coming along to teach me.)

I changed in high school, I really did. I started to grow up. I wasn't the bad Jackson kid any more. I didn't go out looking for trouble. I did my chores in the morning, went to school, went to practice, came home and studied, seriously studied. I liked science and English and math—up to a point. I liked algebra and geometry; I didn't much care for calculus.

More and more, I thought about going to college, about getting an education, learning enough to get out of Bessemer and leave my childhood behind. "I don't know how in hell I'm going to send you," my mom said, "'cause I don't have the money." She wanted me to go to college as badly as I did, she just didn't know how. But I kept talking about it and talking about it, and she began to see that playing sports might get me there.

I love my mom—and I tell her so every day now—but I had trouble telling her when I was younger. I was too busy rebelling, too busy feeling angry and sorry for myself. But she taught me so much. She taught me to do things right, to do them well. "If you're gonna do something," she said, "don't do a half-assed job."

For most of my mom's life, she made beds in motel rooms, and she said that when her supervisor came by, he could bounce a coin off the bed because she put everything she had into making that bed right. She told me that any room she cleaned, you could go in and give it the white-glove test, and your glove would come out clean. Her coworkers would ask her, "Why do you spend so much time making these rooms spotless?" and she'd say, "'Cause that's the way I keep my house. That's the way I'm teaching my kids."

She wanted everything to be perfect.

So do I.

Maybe that's why when I hit a home run or throw out a runner or run for a touchdown, I'm not as impressed as some people seem to be. Because I know I haven't done it *perfect*. I didn't get all of the ball. I had a little too much arc on the throw. I was half a step late hitting the hole. I wasn't perfect.

During my junior and senior years at McAdory, we had pretty good teams in all the sports I played. We didn't go undefeated in football, but we came close. I played fullback and defensive end most of the time, and Keith and Leroy were halfbacks and linebackers. I also did the placekicking. One game my junior year I scored twenty-nine points, ran for three touchdowns, caught a pass for another, kicked a field goal and kicked two extra points. I liked tackling people, too. Once I sacked the quarterback, but as he was going down, he threw a pass and completed it, so I got up and ran down the receiver and tackled him, too. He only gained a couple of yards.

Coach Atchison used to say I never came off the field, but that wasn't true. I came off the field to put on my kicking shoe, and I came off the field to take it off. The rest of the time, I stayed on the field.

I enjoyed the games, but I hated practice. I drove one of the assistant coaches, Johnny Benavidez, crazy. He'd give us something to practice, and I'd just turn and walk off the field, like I was fixing to go to the locker room.

Coach Benavidez couldn't grab me and stop me because I was too much bigger than he was. "Coach Atchison, Coach Atchison," he'd yell, "will you talk to Jackson? He won't listen to me."

Then Coach Atchison would have to come over and talk to me. I was bigger than him, too, but he was the only one I'd listen to. I didn't listen to him all the time. Sometimes he'd try reverse psychology on me. "If you don't want to play, if you don't want to be here," he'd say, "you just get your ass up and leave. We don't need you."

So I'd get my ass up and leave. I didn't want to practice, anyway. All we did was beat on each other. We scrimmaged every day.

My senior year, I weighed more than two hundred pounds, and I ran the forty in about 4.3 seconds, but I still took my turn, sharing the ball-carrying with Leroy and Keith. I only carried about ten or eleven times a game. I averaged about ten or eleven yards a carry. I scored seventeen touchdowns, and I made All-State, but my mom never saw me play, not once. She was afraid she'd see me get hurt.

She almost came to one game. We were playing

our crosstown rival, Jess Lanier High, the Bessemer city school. We were the county school, and we hated each other. My mom could hear the noise from the stadium when she was sitting on her porch. She decided to drive over to the stadium, and when she got close, she heard my name on the P.A. system—I had just scored on a 78-yard run—but she couldn't hear what they were saying about me.

Then she heard a siren, so she figured it was an ambulance and I was hurt, and she turned around and drove home. She never did come in the stadium.

Our school was integrated, and we never had any trouble with prejudice on our team. We'd been playing together since junior high, and we all got along. The only difference was that most of the white kids on the team had their own cars—one guy had a customized Jeep with a picture of Dolly Parton painted under the hood, boobs and all—and only a few of the black kids had cars, most of them like my beat-up old Riviera. My hood had a decoration, too. A big dent in it; that was its decoration.

Our quarterback was a white kid named Steve Mann, and he was ambidextrous—he could pass with either hand. He also pitched on the baseball team, and he would pitch right-handed one inning and left-handed the next. During our senior year, there was some kind of a poll to pick the best athlete in school, or the best student-athlete, and when Steve Mann beat me out, a lot of the black students were really pissed off. "Oh, man, we're not gonna take this," guys told me. "You deserve this award." The black students threatened to boycott classes.

The principal called a meeting of all the seniors in the library, and after a bunch of angry words went back and forth, I stood up and said, "Look, I'm not here to get any awards. I'm here to get an education, to graduate and get the hell out of here. You can all stay here and fight or argue, whatever you want to do, but I'm going back to class."

And I got up and walked out.

That was the end of it. Everybody realized how stupid they were acting, and they all made up. Steve probably deserved the award, anyway. I had good grades, but they weren't as good as Steve's.

After football season each year, I ran indoor track and got myself ready for the outdoor season. We had a great track team. We were always the last team to show up at meets—we could run faster than our assistant coach could drive the bus—and everybody would be wondering, "When are those kids in the ugly gold sweatsuits going to show up?" Once we showed up, everybody else started worrying about second place. We won the state championship my senior year.

I was about 75 percent of the team. I entered five or six events each meet. I set a state record in the triple jump when I was a junior, and I broke it when I was a senior, went close to fifty feet. I also set a state record in the 100-yard dash, 9.5 seconds, something like that. I think I held the record, too, in the hurdles and maybe the long jump. Sometimes I'd win one or two dashes and the hurdles and the high jump, the long jump and the triple jump. I loved to high jump. That's really where I got rid of all my anger—jumping as high as I could.

If I was angry enough, I could jump six-ten or six-eleven pretty regularly in practice. Once, when I was a senior and weighed about two hundred pounds, I cleared seven feet in practice. I was looking forward to breaking the Alabama record in the high jump in the state championships my senior year.

But the triple jump came before the high jump, and as I tried to break my triple-jump record, I twisted my ankle, chipped a bone and had to scratch out of the high jump. That was the most disappointing thing that happened to me in sports in high school. I'm still bitter about it. I was ready to jump seven feet.

I won the state championship in the decathlon in both my junior and senior years. I never did figure out the proper way to throw the discus, but I did get it out around a hundred and fifty feet. And even without practicing the pole vault, I managed to clear twelve feet, which was probably a state record for a black kid. The best part of my two decathlon championships was that both times I was so far ahead I didn't have to run the final event, the mile run. You can have distance running.

In the spring, I competed in track and field and baseball, and if we had both a track meet and a ball game on the same day, I'd pick the one that I thought was more important. Sometimes I'd compete in one sport one day, and the other the next. It gave me an excuse not to have to go to practice.

My junior year, I batted .450 in baseball and won nine out of ten games as a pitcher. I didn't want to pitch—I'd rather throw rocks than a baseball—but one day our coach, Terry Brasseale, saw me, standing flat-footed in center field, throw a ball on the fly over the backstop. "Do you pitch?" he asked me.

"I did," I said, "when I was little. But I don't like to. There's not enough action. It's boring."

But Coach Brasseale wanted me to pitch, so we worked out a rotation: I'd pitch one game, play center field the next to give my arm a rest, play shortstop the next game, then pitch again. I wanted to be playing shortstop and center field all the time.

I wasn't the only one who didn't want me to pitch. The players on the other teams didn't like it, either. I threw too hard. I had a ninety-mile-an-hour fastball in high school. I pitched like Luis Tiant. I faced the outfield and then whirled and threw to home. I had a sinker and a slider. Once I heard one of the parents from the other team say, "Get that man off the mound! He doesn't need to be playing against our kids."

I tried to get out of pitching. Once I even threw sixteen straight balls to the first four batters so that I could be switched to center field. My senior year, I pitched a couple of no-hitters, but I still didn't like it. When we reached the game for the county championship, Coach Brasseale told me, "You're pitching."

"I don't want to pitch," I said.

"You either pitch," he said, "or you don't play."

I pitched, and we won the county championship. I think the score was 6–3.

I batted close to .500 my senior year and I hit twenty home runs in twenty-five games, which tied the national high school record for home runs, even though I missed half a dozen games because I was running in track meets. I really had twenty-one home runs. Once, against Fairfield High, I hit a low line drive that just wouldn't stop. It cleared the fence by about a foot—and then bounced. The umpires called it a ground-rule double. They said the ball bounced *before* it went over the fence.

The same game, I also hit a high, high pop fly to short left field, and the left fielder, who had been backed up to the fence, came running in. He overran the ball. By the time the ball landed—behind him—I was already at second base. By the time he picked the ball up and threw it home, I had scored. It was ruled an inside-the-park home run.

I finished my high school baseball career with something like ninety stolen bases. I was only thrown out once.

The big league scouts all came to watch me play, but I didn't pay much attention to them, except to try to figure out how to avoid them. The scout from the New York Yankees used to come to my house and talk to my mom, but she never let him talk directly to me. The Yankees did draft me, picked me in the second round of the June 1982 draft. Then they offered me $250,000 to sign with them. I asked my mom what she thought and she said, "You go to college. You can have money for a short time, but education is for your whole life."

My mom and I said no to the Yankees. It was easy for me to say no. I'd been poor my whole life. I couldn't miss something I'd never had. I figured the money would be there later. I'd go to college and play two sports or maybe three and increase my value. Then I'd pick one sport and play it professionally. Or maybe I'd pick two sports and play both of them professionally. I never told anyone that I might play two sports professionally. They would've laughed at me.

I could've had my choice of several colleges. I got my first recruiting letter from Indiana. The Hoosiers. They sent me an Indiana pen. Then the letters started pouring in from everywhere, as far away as UCLA. Then the coaches and the alumni began calling me. It got so bad we just took the phone off the hook. Some of the people who called said, flat-out, "We'll take care of you. We'll take care of your mother. Don't worry about anything." But I got the feeling they would say absolutely anything to get me interested. Some of them probably meant it, and some were just bullshitting.

Maybe if I'd followed sports more when I was a kid, I would've been impressed by some of the schools, or at least been interested enough to go look at them. But I never heard of half the schools. I just wanted to stay near home, near my mom and my family. I'd been out of Alabama only once in my life. When I was eighteen, my high school girlfriend's church sponsored a trip to the Six Flags amusement park in Georgia, and I bought tickets for her and me. "Look, I'm not leaving the state," I told recruiters. "There's nothing you can say to make me leave the state."

Once that message got around, Alabama and Auburn, the two big schools in the state, really started calling, going head-to-head. The University of Alabama was in Tuscaloosa, just a forty-five-minute drive from Bessemer. Auburn was about a hundred miles southeast of us, a two-hour drive. Bobby Wallace recruited me for Auburn, and when he came to get me for my visit to the campus, they sent up a private plane, a two-engine prop plane. They gave me my first plane ride, and it was a blast. I fell in love with flying.

Alabama didn't send a plane for me. Tuscaloosa was too close. But Bear Bryant, the Alabama coach, called me himself. In Alabama, that was almost like getting a call from God. I was a "Roll, Tide!" fan myself; they were the national champions when I was in high school. I went over to Tuscaloosa on a Saturday and met Bear Bryant and went up in his famous tower with him while the Tide was practicing. "Bo, we'd love to have you here," he said in his raspy voice. "We think you could help us in a lot of ways. Offense or defense."

Defense? Right away, I became less of an Alabama fan. The way I figured it, if I went there, they were going to make me into a linebacker. I didn't want that. I wanted to run with the ball.

Ken Donahue, the coach who was recruiting me for Alabama, told me that as a running back, I probably wouldn't play at all my freshman year and maybe just a little my sophomore year. He said they had some great runners, like Major Ogilvie, who had just finished, and Ricky Moore, who had led the team in rushing as a freshman, and I'd just have to wait my turn.

The more I heard, the less I liked the idea of going to Alabama. I visited Auburn, and I liked what Pat Dye, their new coach, said to me. "If you come to Auburn," he said, "I'm not gonna give you anything. You got to earn it. Don't expect to be put up on a pedestal. You've got to work your ass off. But if you do, the accolades will come, the pros will look at you and you will be compensated. The one thing Auburn can give you is a good education."

The more I heard, the more I liked the idea of going to Auburn. Coach Dye said he wouldn't mind my playing baseball or running track in the spring. The Tigers seemed to want me a lot more than Alabama did. Maybe it was because Auburn hadn't beaten Alabama in nine years.

One day in the spring, I came home from a baseball game, and Pat Dye and Bobby Wallace were in the house, talking to my mom. She had given them coffee and some tea cakes, and I was very quiet, I just said, "Hi," and "'Bye," and went downstairs, took my baseball uniform out of my duffel bag and put it in with the laundry. I heard someone coming downstairs, and it was Coach Dye. "Bo," he said, "I just came down to ask you. Are you coming to Auburn?"

"Yes, I am," I said.

"All right," he said. "That's all I wanted to know."

I told him not to tell anybody yet, but he had my word, and my word was good. On the day I signed the letter of intent to go to Auburn, Bobby Wallace flew up from Auburn in a helicopter, landed on a hill down the street from my house and everybody in the neighborhood came out to look. It was the first time a helicopter ever landed in our neighborhood.

The news cameras came out and took pictures of me signing to go to Auburn, and there were headlines in Birmingham, saying that Auburn had beaten Alabama in the recruiting war. But the people from Alabama said it didn't matter, Auburn still wasn't going to beat Alabama where it counted, on the football field. Ken Donahue, the coach who had recruited me for Alabama, said that Bo Jackson could look forward to losing to Alabama for the next four years.

By the time I graduated from McAdory, there were stories going around about how much Auburn was paying me to go to school there. You know: "Bo Jackson is going to Auburn because his mother is now the proud owner of a chain of 7-Eleven stores"—or "Bo's mom now drives a new Cadillac."

I've got a pretty good idea where those stories were coming from.

Not from the University of Alabama.

I think they were coming from the Yankees. I think somebody at the New York Yankees was trying to get me in trouble, trying to force me to turn pro. I know the Yankees were unhappy because I'd passed up their offer.

Besides, the man who owns the Yankees, George Steinbrenner, didn't like the idea of me going to Auburn. He lives in Florida, and he's a University of Florida and Florida State fan. Auburn played both of them every year. Steinbrenner told a sportswriter I know that if I passed up all the money he offered me, Auburn had to be paying me a fortune.

Auburn wasn't paying me anything. If I'd gotten any payoff, the first thing I would've done was help out my mother, and she was still living in the same house and still making beds and cleaning motel rooms.

Somebody spread the story that I was driving a brand-new $40,000 sports car. I still had the 1967 Riviera with the crooked hood and no muffler.

I did get a color TV set—from my father. He gave it to me the day I left for Auburn. I took off with just my clothing and my color TV set, and a burning desire never to come back to Bessemer, except for visits.

Even four days after the fight, Bo Jackson was still stunned, still in pain. "I couldn't sleep that night," he recalled. "I'm serious. I tossed and turned, and in the morning, I looked in the paper to see if I was dreaming, or if it really happened. It happened. Mike Tyson lost."

Bo stood on the deck in back of his Kansas home with a new bow in his hands, flexing it, testing its strength. Inside, his wife prepared lunch, and his children played, the house filled with toys, the garage with cars—suburbia incarnate. "I felt like *I* lost," Bo said, "because here's a guy that's just like me."

He picked up an arrow, fixed it, drew back the bow and fired. The arrow whistled into the ground in back of Bo's home. "I was so into Mike Tyson," he said. "The guy is young, grew up with nothing just like me, a hoodlum, a gangster, and then he's on top of the world. He had the whole world believing, 'Hey, I'm not gonna get beat, not ever. I refuse to get beat.' That's how I am. I refuse to get beat at anything."

But Tyson, Bo was reminded, spent his teens in a juvenile prison; Bo did not. "But if I lived where he lived," Bo said, "I probably would've been worse. I probably would've been the guy that bullied Mike Tyson around. Believe me. When he lost, I lost."

Bo put down the bow and settled into a deck chair. "I am still that mean-assed person deep down inside," he said. "There is still that Jason in me."

Jason is the indestructible evil force in the *Friday the 13th* films.

"I refuse to let him get out of his box," Bo said. "I refuse to let him get out of his cage. Except on Sundays in the fall. I let him out on Sundays when I strap my helmet on and go out and play football."

Bo paused and thought for a moment. "But once in a while," he said, "he sneaks out. A couple of years ago, on a rainy day, we were taking batting practice in the cage under the stands. One of the guys was mouthing off—he had gotten a big hit the night before—and he jumped into the batting cage first. When he finished, and the next guy jumped in, I decided to go back to the locker room and put on my gym shorts.

"When I came back, the second guy was finishing, and it was my turn. I was just coming through the door, and the first guy sees me and jumps into the cage. 'Excuse me,' I said, 'but didn't you just take your turn?'

" 'Well, you shoulda been here,' he said. 'You missed your turn. You gotta be ready.'

"He was trying to show me up in front of the coaches. I said, 'Look, man, will you just shut up and get out of the cage? I am not about to stand here and watch you take a second round of BP when I haven't had my first.'

"I moved into the cage, and he backed out. But he kept mouthing off at me. 'You're pissing me off,' I told him. 'You better shut your mouth, or I'm gonna kick your ass.'

"The batting practice pitcher threw the first pitch, and I swung and missed, and I was pissed off, and the guy said something again, something smart-ass. I slammed the bat down, and before he could blink, I leaped out of the cage, grabbed him around the throat with my left hand, lifted him off the ground and slammed his head against the wall. It sounded like a bat hit the wall.

"His eyes rolled back in his head, and I started talking. 'Look, you picked the wrong motherfucker to mess with on the wrong day. As long as you're breathing air, don't you ever talk to me like that again.'

"The coaches were so shocked they didn't know what to do. They just stood there because I always make the rule, first day of the year, that if anybody tries to stop me from kicking someone's ass, I'm gonna turn on them like a pit bull.

"Finally, four of the coaches jumped me and pulled my hands off the guy's neck, and he just slid to the floor. They took him to the training room and put ice on him, and I went to my locker and took my bat and hit my locker as hard as I could, I was still so mad. I got madder and madder—so mad because he brought the Jason out of me— and I jumped up and ran to the training room and stood over him and said, 'Don't you ever cross me again. If you do, I'm not gonna give those coaches time. I'm gonna rip your ass.'

"Later, when he got his senses back, he came to my locker and said, 'Look, let's just forget about what happened, and let's be friends,' and I said, 'No, the shit don't work that way. You meant what you said when you said it.' "

Bo fights a constant war against his anger, a fight he does not always win. "I don't take no shit off nobody," he said, the anger still stabbing him, "and it's not because I'm Bo Jackson. It's just if I'm going to be a man, if I'm going to be a husband to my wife and a father to my children, how can I let somebody talk to me like I'm anything less?"

Bo stopped, and then, in the silence, the fury with which he had recalled the batting cage incident subsided. "If nobody messes with me," he said finally, "I don't mess with them."

He managed to smile. "Sometimes I wish I could go back to my childhood," he said. "I wish I could be twelve years old again. I wish that for two or three hours each day I could go back and be that nappy-haired rock-chunking hoodlum I used to be."

The smile widened, the tension eased. Bo knew how far he had come. He was a grown-up again, an adult, mature and temperate, and he knew what that meant. "You can't pick your nose in public and flick boogers on your buddies," he said.

3 SET YOUR GOALS HIGH—AND DON'T STOP

was scared when I arrived at Auburn. I was afraid I wouldn't fit in. I was afraid I wouldn't make the team. I'd never been away from home before, and I'd never competed against players as good as the players at Auburn. But I got over my fears pretty quick.

In the summer of 1982, I went to school half a day and worked half a day. I studied history and geography, and I painted yellow lines in the parking lot in one of the malls. It was a hundred and twenty degrees in the parking lot. But I hated history even worse. It was a relief when football practice began.

The day we started two-a-day practices, I met a girl and began sowing my wild oats. I'd practice in the morning, run over to her place, get laid, come back, eat lunch, practice in the afternoon and run back to her place.

I don't know how many times I got laid that first week—I've never been real good on stats—but I bet I set an Auburn record. Maybe a national collegiate record. I still had plenty of energy for practice. I was only nineteen.

I wasn't supposed to be the top running back in the freshman class. Alan Evans was. He was a blue-chipper, the cream of the crop. He came from south Alabama, and in high school he ranked right up with Marcus Dupree from Mississippi. They were rated the two best high school running backs in the South.

Evans was a roger-dodger type, a dancer. He'd dodge you, but he didn't have great speed. The first time we ran a forty, I beat him easily. I beat everyone on the team.

The coaches at first wanted me to play fullback. In Coach Dye's wishbone offense, the fullback was the blocking back. "I didn't come here to get down on all fours and be a damn blocking back," I told the coaches. "I came here to be a running back."

They put me at running back, and in our first scrimmage I ran right over a big defensive tackle, Donnie Humphrey, just plowed over him and went for a touchdown. Humphrey was All-Southeastern Conference, the meanest man on the team. He later played for the Green Bay Packers. "If I can run over him," I said to myself, "I can run over anyfuckingbody."

My first roommate was a lineman, a nasty guy, a slob. He used to leave his socks and his jockstraps lying all around the room. I couldn't take it. I like things neat. After a week, I said, "Get your ass out of here," and from then on, I roomed with Tommie Agee.

I roomed with Tommie for four years, and I love him like a brother. He had the skinniest legs on the whole team—and the strongest. He could leg-press damn near a ton, almost two thousand pounds. On third and two, we'd give him the ball up the middle and he'd tow four or five guys six yards with those powerful skinny legs of his.

Tommie got redshirted our freshman year—he twisted a knee and sat out the season—but for the next three years he played fullback and blocked for me. He didn't just block people. He hurt them. He made them wonder whether they really wanted to tackle *anybody*. Tommie was the main reason I won the Heisman Trophy my senior year.

My freshman season, I used to walk past the Heisman every day, the one Pat Sullivan won in 1971, the only one ever won by an Auburn player. I'd look at Pat's trophy and I'd see my name on it. I told the girl I was dating I had two goals at Auburn: to win the Heisman Trophy and to be picked first in the NFL draft. I didn't tell anyone else. In fact, by the time I was a senior, I was telling people what I was supposed to tell them, that the thought of winning the Heisman Trophy had never even crossed my mind.

I didn't start the opening game against Wake Forest. But I went in early, and Lionel James, The Little Train, a five-foot-six running back who was a junior, turned to me and said, "When we pitch you the ball, haul ass! Don't stop till you get to the end zone!"

The first play they pitched me the ball, I hauled ass so hard I ran right into a defender. All I had to do was cut to his left or to his right and I would've gone 80-something yards for a touchdown. But the third or fourth time I ran the ball, I went around end and went 44 yards for a touchdown. I carried the ball a total of ten times and gained more than 100 yards and scored two touchdowns, and from then on, as long as I was healthy, I was in the starting lineup.

I discovered right after the first game that I had a lot of new friends at Auburn, people who wanted to get to know me and do things for me. "Want to come to the frat house? Want to borrow my car? My truck? Come to a party?"

I stuck with the friends I already had, friends from the team, like Tommie Agee and Lionel James and Tim Jessie. Lionel lived in the same suite that Tommie and I did. Tim lived on a different floor, but he hung out in our suite. He was also a running back, also a freshman. We were all country boys and our idea of a good time was to go to Kentucky Fried Chicken and get a barrel of chicken and go to Cap'n D's and get a box of fish and pick up a bunch of sodas and go to the park or go fishing.

We never got in trouble, never broke curfew, never went looking for fights. We were all happy to be in college, content, grateful. We knew we were popular, knew kids looked up to us, and we didn't want to scar our reputations by having people say they saw us out after curfew or saw us getting drunk or getting into a fight.

We liked being role models, and we grew together at Auburn, we had fun together. Even though we saw each other just about every day for four years, I don't think we ever had an argument—not a serious one. Nobody had a big head. Nobody had an attitude. When it was all over, we hugged and told each other how much we loved each other, and then we pretty much went our separate ways. We all ended up in the NFL, but on different teams.

I don't mean to say we never had problems in

college. The first year was the hardest. I didn't like practice any more than I liked it in high school, and I guess I showed it. The Auburn coaching staff believed fervently in hard workouts, and the coach for the running backs, Bud Casey, didn't think I was working hard enough. One day he yelled at me and grabbed my face mask. I shook off his hand so fast he thought he'd been shot. "Don't you ever do that again!" I told him. "Don't you ever grab me again!" He never did.

I was still stuttering, still reluctant to talk to the media, but I was having a good freshman season, and some people were starting to compare me to Georgia's Herschel Walker, who was on his way to winning the Heisman Trophy that year. I got sick of hearing Herschel's name, sick of the attention and the pressure, and then, in the next-to-last game of the season, Georgia beat us and clinched the SEC championship, and Herschel had a good game and I didn't play very well.

I was frustrated, I was depressed, I was tired. I wasn't used to a football season lasting so long. I wanted to go home.

About six o'clock on a Friday night, the week before the biggest game of the season, the Alabama game, I went over to the Greyhound bus depot in Opelika, the town next to Auburn, and I sat there for hours, all by myself, while seven or eight buses left for Birmingham. "I'll catch the next one," I told myself each time a Birmingham bus pulled out.

But then each time I'd think, "My mom's proud of me. My brothers and sisters are proud of me. What'll they think if I quit? What'll I do? Go home and hang around the neighborhood? Be like so many other guys, doing nothing? I don't want to be *nothing*. I want to be *something*."

"Either buy a ticket and get on a bus," the man who was cleaning up the depot said to me, "or you gotta leave."

It was after one o'clock in the morning. I called Bobby Wallace, the coach who had recruited me, and told him where I was and what I was thinking of doing. I called him because I knew he'd talk me out of leaving.

"Come back to the dorm," Coach Wallace said. "We'll have a talk."

We sat at a picnic table outside Sewell Hall, the athletic dormitory, and we talked till close to four o'clock in the morning. We talked about success and failure, trying and quitting. I felt better. I didn't even mind when Coach Wallace told me I'd have to run a hundred "stadiums" for being out after curfew: up and down the steps at Jordan-Hare Stadium a hundred times.

Then we played Alabama. I ran 53 yards on one play, which matched my longest run of the year, and with less than three minutes to play, and Alabama leading, 22–17, on fourth down and goal to go at the one-yard line, I took the ball and dove for the end zone.

As I was hit, I looked down and saw the goal line and saw that I wasn't past it, and I stretched out and stuck the ball into the end zone, and I looked down the line at the official and he threw his hands up in the air, signaling a touchdown. We won, 23–22. It was Auburn's first victory over Alabama in ten years.

I looked over at the sidelines and I saw Bear Bryant and he looked like someone had walked along and stepped on his sandcastle. Then I looked at Ken Donahue, the assistant coach, the one who'd told me I'd have to wait at least a year to play at Alabama, the one who said Auburn would never beat the Tide. He looked like he had just swallowed a wad of shit. I took off my helmet and walked off the field.

A few weeks later, we played in the Tangerine Bowl, in Orlando against Boston College and Doug Flutie, who would win the Heisman Trophy in 1984. In fact, during my freshman season, I played against the next three Heisman winners: Herschel, Mike Rozier of Nebraska and Flutie.

My mom got a scare the week before the Tangerine Bowl. One of our linebackers, a guy named Beau Brown, got in some trouble in a topless bar in Orlando, and when my mom heard that someone named Beau had been sent home, she nearly had a heart attack. I told her not to worry, that my only problem was back spasms. "If your back's hurting," she said, "don't you go out there and play. Don't let anyone pressure you into playing."

By then, she had become a fan. The Auburn people had talked her into coming to the opening game and had treated her like a queen, and once she saw seventy thousand people packed into Jordan-Hare Stadium, all of them going wild when her son ran onto the field, she was hooked. She didn't miss a game I played at Auburn.

When we went out on the field to stretch before the Boston College game, my back was still aching. But after I looked up in the stands and saw my mom, and she waved to me, the pain went away. I played and ran for two touchdowns, and we beat Boston College. I made All-Southeastern Conference in football, then went right to the indoor track season.

After just two weeks of practice, I ran the sixty in 6.18 seconds in the LSU Invitational. It was the fourth-fastest time in Auburn history, and two of the other three guys, Harvey Glance and Stanley Floyd, were Olympic-class sprinters. I ran track the rest of the winter, earned my letter, then switched to baseball in the spring. The best part of being a three-sport athlete was that I didn't have to play spring football. The only thing worse than practicing football in the fall is practicing football in the spring.

Again, I only had a couple of weeks of practice, then began playing baseball games, and I guess I didn't have my batting eye at first. I struck out my first twenty-one times up. I wondered if I was ever going to hit the ball again. But then I settled down, batted .400 the rest of the season, hit a few home runs, played center field and got my letter in baseball, too.

They told me I was the first three-sport letterman in the Southeastern Conference in twenty years, the first at Auburn in thirty years. I didn't think much about it. After all, I was only a freshman.

That year, I studied what they called GC, a general curriculum course. The athletic department assigned an academic adviser to me, and he meant well, but he had a tendency to pick out courses he thought I wouldn't have any trouble passing. He was more worried about my eligibility than my education. After my freshman year, I switched to a new academic adviser. I wanted to take courses so that I could learn something. For my sophomore year, I enrolled in almost all psychology courses.

During the summer between my freshman and sophomore years, I worked as a teller at the Colonial Bank in Birmingham. My first day on the job, I balanced my books and came up $15,000 short. I was a little worried at first—even if the president of the bank was an Auburn trustee—but after my coworkers helped me figure out that the money wasn't really missing, I was able to kid about it. "It was a rookie mistake," I said.

The most exciting part of the summer was driving to work each day on the interstate. Once, a woman driving in front of me lost control, hit another car and swerved into a guardrail. I was the second person to stop. I saw that the woman was hurt, that her head was bleeding and that smoke was coming out of the hood and gas was leaking from the back.

"We better get her out before this explodes," I said. We lifted her out, and moved her away from the smoking car, and when the police and the paramedics showed up, I just got in my car and drove off.

Another day, I accidentally smacked into the back of a woman's car, and she stopped and jumped out, all angry and worked up, ready to snap at me till she heard my name. "You play football for Auburn?" she said.

"Yes, ma'am," I said.

"Are you all right?" she said.

A few months later, before our second game of the season, she sent me a telegram at school: SMASH TEXAS LIKE YOU SMASHED MY CAR.

We had a great football team my sophomore year, a great season. I ran for more than 1,000 yards, Lionel ran for more than 700 and Tommie ran for more than 600. Among us, we *averaged* almost 7 yards a carry.

That was the year I made up my mind it was better to give a lick than to receive one. My own Golden Rule. I realized that the defensive guys always tried to hit the running backs as hard as they could, to punish them, to warn them not to run their way again. Until my sophomore year, I had always tried to avoid the punishment. I had tried to run around the defensive men. When I didn't get around them, they knocked the hell out of me. I really didn't know how to get down and lower my shoulder and explode on them. But my sophomore year, I learned. If anybody got in my way, I tried my best to run right through him. I tried to put a big hole in him.

We lost only one game, the Texas game, and as much as it went against Coach Dye's grain, he realized that if he and his staff didn't push me in practice, just let me get ready at my own pace, then I'd produce on Saturday. I didn't let him down.

My mom became an expert on football, a regular Howard Cosell. "You know, when you go around end, and those guys are trying to hit you low," she said, "you just jump over them, that's what you do." My mom.

I was still sowing my wild oats. Getting laid Friday night, the night before the game, was a ritual for me. And sometimes I'd get up real early Saturday morning, run across campus, get laid and then get back to Sewell Hall before anybody else got up. I got all that out of my system in college. I got all that out of my system before I got married. Now, every town I go to, women come chasing after me, calling my room, sending me notes, but I don't pay them any attention. I wouldn't want any woman who chases after me, and I stopped chasing after them once I taught my wife how to fire my pistol.

My other ritual at Auburn was falling asleep before each game. Other guys would get all pumped up in the locker room, some of them banging their heads against the wall, some of them throwing up. I'd be yawning. The closer we got to the game, the sleepier I got. It had nothing to do with my other pregame ritual. As soon as I got on the field and somebody hit me, I woke up.

I saved my best game for Alabama, the best game of my college career. We played in a storm, with tornadoes whipping through the state, and I carried the ball twenty times and gained 256 yards. It was my first 200-yard game. I average 12.8 yards a carry, the most I averaged for any game in four years. I scored two touchdowns, the first on a 69-yard run, the second on a 71-yard run that brought us from behind to beat the Tide, 23–20, clinch the Southeastern Conference championship and put us in the Sugar Bowl to play Michigan.

I got a lot of attention for a sophomore, and the owner of the Baltimore Colts, Robert Irsay, started talking about how he was thinking of signing me for $2.5 million. Herschel had cut his college career short to sign with the USFL, the new league, and Irsay said he could get me to sign with the NFL. It was a bunch of bullshit—I never met the man, never talked to him, never had any contact with him, directly or indirectly—and the NCAA looked into it and decided that he was just shooting off his mouth and embarrassing me.

I had already turned my back on $1 million. Some guys had walked up to me in the Laundromat, told me they were getting a franchise for a new USFL team in Florida and showed me a $1 million cashier's check and a contract. All I had to do, they said, was sign the contract and take the check. I don't know who they were, or where they got the money, but I could tell from working in the bank that the check was real. I told them they were crazy.

I didn't want their million. I didn't want Irsay's

money. I wanted to stay in school. I was having too much fun.

Before the Sugar Bowl, we worked out in the Superdome in New Orleans, and some of the guys tried to see if they could kick a ball hard enough and high enough to hit the scoreboard hanging from the roof. Nobody could. It was more than fifty yards straight up. But I picked up a football and hit the middle of the scoreboard on my second try. I always could throw pretty well.

(Once I had a football throwing contest with Pat Washington, one of our quarterbacks. He threw the ball more than eighty yards on the fly, and I threw it more than a hundred.)

I took a pounding in the Sugar Bowl. Michigan had the toughest, hardest-hitting little white guys I ever saw. They were like bees; they just kept stinging you. One guy would hit you and fall off, and then another would hit you. I couldn't believe how sore I was at the end. But we won, 9–7, and when they tried to name me the Most Valuable Player, I gave the trophy to Lionel James. It was the last game of his college career, the last time we'd be playing together, and it was my way of saying, "Thank you for helping me get through my first two years at Auburn." He was like a big brother to me, a five-foot-six big brother. He deserved to be MVP, not me. I thought he played a more physical game than I did.

After the Sugar Bowl, I decided to pass up baseball for a year and concentrate on track and field, to see if I could make the United States Olympic team as a sprinter. I ran some fast hundreds, but not quite fast enough to qualify for the Olympic trials. I never did get to run against Carl Lewis. But I still think that if

I'd had the time to really work on my sprinting, if I had lost twenty pounds, if I had gotten down under two hundred, I could've beaten Carl. In the sprints—not in the long jump. (During the summer of 1984, while Carl was winning four gold medals for sprinting and jumping in the Olympic Games, I won a few medals for sprinting and jumping, too—in the Alabama Sports Festival.)

When spring football came to an end, with the traditional intrasquad game, I took part—but not in the game. Instead, I ran a pregame race against a few hundred local youngsters. I offered to buy dinner for anyone who could beat me goal to goal—and I spotted them all fifteen yards. I didn't even have to buy one burger.

A few days later, I went out to the lake with Tommie Agee and Tim Jessie and a freshman running back named Brent Fullwood. We decided to go fishing in a twelve-foot johnboat. Tommie said he'd wait on shore; he didn't know how to swim. I rowed, and Brent and Tim fished. I helped Tim put some twelve-pound test line on his reel, and he caught a few fish, swung them past my head, bragged about his casting. After we'd been out for about forty-five minutes—*pow!*—something hit me in the head. I thought I'd been shot.

I opened my eyes and saw a fishing line dangling in front of me, blowing in the wind. I looked out in the water and saw half a fishing pole starting to sink. I reached up to my head and felt a fishing lure with its hook sticking into me. "Oh Lord," Tim said, "I didn't mean to do that."

Brent looked at the lure sticking out of my head and he started to laugh, and then Tim began laughing, too, and I said, "If you two don't shut up, I'm gonna turn this boat over and drown you both right here in the lake." I rowed to shore, and Tommie, who was waiting there, saw what had happened and shouted, "Hey, Tim, I see you caught you a bigmouth bass!"

They all thought it was funny as hell. They cut the line, but left the hook in my head and told me I'd have to go to the hospital to get it taken out. I didn't want to go to the Auburn hospital because I figured I'd be recognized and the story would get around, so we went to the county hospital, to the emergency room. It was busy. A kid had jumped in a creek and cut off part of his heel on a pipe; someone had cut up his arm in a kitchen accident. I had my baseball hat on, tilted sideways, like the gangsters wear them, to cover up the lure. I walked up to the receptionist, a woman sitting behind a little window, and she said, "What seems to be the problem?"

"Well, I got something stuck in my head," I said.

She said, "What?" and I said, "A fishing lure," and she said, "Did you pull it out?" and I said, "No." One of the doctors standing behind her saw me and said, "That's Bo Jackson," and then he said, "Well, where's the lure?" and I lifted my cap, and I guess it looked pretty funny, a fishing lure poking out of my head, and he started laughing, and then a few more people recognized me, and they laughed, too, and soon everybody in the waiting room, even the people who were cut up, was laughing.

The doctor took me in back and shot me with some kind of painkiller and got the hook out and put on some ointment and sent me home, and the next day the newspaper had a story about Tim Jessie catching a world-record bass.

By the end of my sophomore year, I'd had enough of psychology, so I switched my major to family and child development in the School of Human Sciences. I got credit for most of my psychology courses, and finally I felt I was where I belonged. I could learn about kids—which really interested me—and, at the same time, I could try to figure out why I was the type of kid I was: angry and aggressive and jealous.

I worked with the kids at the Auburn Child Development Center. Just my being there seemed to make some of the troubled kids feel better, and that made me feel good. I've never been able to figure out why I've been blessed in so many ways, why athletic success has come so easy to me, and why so many other people have to struggle so hard every day of their lives. I try to let them know that there's someone out there who cares, someone besides their loved ones. If I can get a child who's in pain—physically or mentally—to smile, if I can brighten his day, that's better than hitting a home run, better than scoring a touchdown. That makes me feel like I've actually done something worthwhile.

Auburn didn't give me grades. I studied. If Auburn had been giving me grades, I'd have my degree by now. Instead, I'm still a handful of credits short, but I'm going to keep going back until I earn my degree. I promised my mom and I promised myself. "I am going to go to school, get my education and play the hell out of some ball while I'm there," I said years ago, and I meant it.

Some athletes go to college and don't learn any-thing—sometimes because the school doesn't care, sometimes because the athlete doesn't care. At Auburn, the school cared—up to a point. They checked up on the athletes, tried to make sure that everybody at least went to classes. But not all the athletes cared. Some of them are still hanging around Auburn, years later. That's all they do, hang around; they're like old furniture. I see them every year when I go back.

I hate failure. I *hate* it.

I blame the athletes when they don't care enough to get an education—and I blame the athletes when the school doesn't care, too. I don't think there really are dumb people, but there are misguided people, misled people. Too many athletes allow colleges to mislead them, *misuse* them. It takes the dignity out of college athletics when you have a guy playing football who can't spell football.

I feel bad for Dexter Manley of the Washington Redskins, coming out of college illiterate. It's truly sad. They didn't care if he made A's or B's or even learned to read. The only thing they cared about was him getting out on Saturday and ripping somebody's head off. But he let them do that to him. It's Dexter's own fault. He let them mislead him, persuade him that playing football was all that mattered.

I cared. I refused to let anyone at Auburn mislead me. I was not going to sit there and play ball and take badminton and sewing classes, just to be eligible.

I made *Playboy* magazine's preseason All-American team in 1984, and so did one of our linebackers, Gregg Carr. They flew both of us to Dallas for photographs and a TV special, and even though I didn't meet any bunnies or any Playmates—I don't think the NCAA would've gone for that—I had a good time. I did meet Gil Brandt, who was the vice president of the Dallas Cowboys, and he told me that if I signed with

Dallas after I finished my college career, they'd give me the stadium. "What would I want with a stadium with a hole in the roof?" I said.

When the season started, I was one of the favorites to win the Heisman Trophy, along with Flutie and Napoleon McCallum of Navy, who were both seniors. We opened our season in the Kickoff Classic in New Jersey, playing Miami, the defending national champions, and I gained almost 100 yards rushing. But I played most of the second half with a twisted ankle, and we lost, by two points. The next game, we faced Texas, the only team to beat us the year before.

In the third quarter, with the score tied, I broke loose, got into the clear, nobody between me and the goal line. Jerry Gray, Texas's All-American safety, took off after me, but once I get a step, if I'm running right, no way in hell anybody catches me from behind. But Gray caught me. I wasn't running right. My ankle was hurting.

Gray caught up to me and jumped on my back and rolled me down after a 53-yard run. The artificial turf at Memorial Stadium in Austin was so hard it was like a sidewalk painted green. I hit shoulder-first, and the pain shot through my whole body. I went numb, but I wasn't coming out of the game, not when we had a chance to beat Texas. I played seven more plays, carried the ball a couple of times and threw a few blocks, and when I realized I couldn't lift my right arm—I couldn't even move it—I came out of the game. I had a shoulder separation—torn ligaments in my right shoulder.

We lost the game, and when we got back to Auburn, they took me to the hospital, and the doctors told me they were going to have to operate on me, my season was finished. I cried like a baby. There was some talk about petitioning the NCAA to give me an extra year of eligibility because of the injury—Donnie Humphrey got an extra year like that—but I wouldn't even consider it. I was going to be twenty-three years old, almost twenty-four, after four years at Auburn. If I stayed an extra year, I would be almost twenty-five when I started a professional career. No way.

Strangely, the shoulder injury turned out to be a good thing for me in several ways. In the first place, it forced me to rest my ankle. If I hadn't hurt the shoulder, I might've kept playing, and I might've messed up my ankle or, favoring it, messed up my knee.

In the second place, with my right arm in a sling, I didn't have to go to practice, so I had a few chances to go home, to visit my growing army of nieces and nephews. For twenty or thirty dollars I could take a dozen of them to Burger King and be a hero. I also got to see my mom, which saved her money on her phone bill, because when I was in school, I always called collect.

And in the third place, I met Linda while I was recuperating. We probably would've met anyway—I had my eye on her for a while, and I think she had hers on me, too—but without practice to keep me busy, we had time to become friends. It was worth getting hurt, just for that.

It was frustrating being hurt. It got to the point where I even missed practicing. I wasn't used to having so much idle time. I called Napoleon McCallum at Navy to compare injuries—he'd broken his leg—and we both said it felt funny just going to classes. I called Doug Flutie at Boston College and wished him good luck, and good health, in the Heisman race. And I called Jerry Gray at Texas, the guy who'd tackled me from behind, and disguised my voice and told him that

I was his agent and I was going to negotiate a pro contract for him. He couldn't figure out who was calling. Finally I told him, and we both laughed. I knew he wasn't trying to hurt me.

I only missed six games. The first game back, against Florida, I carried the ball only five times. The second game back, against Cincinnati, I carried the ball only eight times, but I scored three touchdowns. I went back into the starting lineup for the last two games of the regular season, against Georgia and Alabama.

Against Alabama, I was healthy enough to carry the ball twenty-two times—the only game all year in which I had more than twenty carries. I ran for 118 yards and a touchdown, but I messed up on the play that cost us the game.

In the closing minutes, with us trailing by two points, fourth down on the Alabama one-yard line, I didn't hear the signals at the line of scrimmage. Or I heard them wrong. Coach Dye called for Brent Fullwood to carry the ball, to the weak side, the right side, with me leading him, blocking for him. I went *left*, Brent went right, Alabama stopped him and we lost, 17–15.

The defeat cost us a return trip to the Sugar Bowl. We had to settle for the Liberty Bowl in Memphis.

Some people called me stupid for running the wrong way, and called Coach Dye stupid for not going for a field goal. There were a lot of jokes about my wrong-way run, and even I had to laugh at some of them. My favorite:

Q. How do you get to Memphis?

A. Go to the Alabama one-yard line and turn left.

We beat Arkansas in the Liberty Bowl, and I

scored two of our three touchdowns and won the MVP Award, but it didn't make up for losing to the Tide.

After football season, I decided to skip track, even though it was still my favorite sport, and concentrate on baseball. I figured I had a better chance of making a living in baseball than in track. We had a new coach at Auburn, Hal Baird, who used to pitch in the Kansas City Royals' farm system, and after a year off from the game, I wanted to have a good season.

Early in the season, we went to Georgia for the first night game ever played on their field. A good crowd turned out, and they were on me, riding me about running the wrong way and losing the game against Alabama. When I grounded out my first time up, the fans chanted, "Roll, Tide!" I smiled. As long as it's not my home crowd, I like the fans to get on me. I take it out on the ball.

The second time up, I hit a ball that sailed over the left-center-field fence at the 385-foot mark and hit the lights on top of a tower 85 feet high. Somebody figured out that the ball would've traveled close to 600 feet if it hadn't hit the light tower. The next two times I batted, I hit two more home runs, both to right field, and the Georgia crowd cheered for me each time. The fifth time up, my last time up, I hit a ball that hit the top of the fence, three or four inches short of being a home run. I only got a double. And the fans booed.

I looked up at the press box, and Vince Dooley, the Georgia football coach at the time, was sitting there, shaking his head, as if he were saying, "I don't believe this kid. First he whips our asses in football, and now he whips our asses in baseball."

We stayed overnight at Georgia, and the next day the pitcher who served up my first home run came up to me and handed me a baseball and said, "This is the one you hit off of me last night. Would you sign it for me?" And I did.

I used to entertain my teammates by catching flies with my bare hands—not fly balls, *flies*. If we saw a fly in the cafeteria, I'd reach out and grab it and take it outside and let it go. Once we were having a cookout, and I spotted a whole bunch of flies on a wall, eight or ten of them, all of them within a foot of each other. I turned to our left fielder, Trey Gainous, and I said, "I bet I could catch six of them at one time."

"No way," he said.

I walked up to the wall and went *swack!* and, with my fist clenched, said to Trey, "You think I got 'em?"

"Hell no," he said.

I opened one finger, my little finger, and one fly flew out. I opened the next finger, and two more flew out. I opened the middle finger. Two more. That made five. One more finger to open.

I looked at Trey, and he shook his head. I opened the final finger, and the fly just sat there, the sixth fly.

During the baseball season, I received the Southland Olympia Award, which was presented to outstanding amateur athletes, most of them Olympic champions, like Carl Lewis and Greg Louganis and Mary Lou Retton. Bob Mathias and Rafer Johnson, who were both Olympic decathlon champions, were among the people who chose the winners, and I liked what they said about me. "He seems like a young man who has his academic, athletic and social priorities in order," Mathias said. "He is a great athlete, a fine student and a person eager to give of himself to others," Johnson said. They gave me a Greek vase to add to all my plaques and trophies.

I ended the season batting over .400 with seventeen home runs in forty-two games, and nine stolen bases in ten attempts. I was timed in 3.9 seconds getting from the batter's box to first base, which is supposed to be pretty fast, and I threw a few pitches, just for fun, that were timed at close to ninety miles an hour, which meant my shoulder was healed. People who saw a lot of college baseball compared me to Will Clark of Mississippi State and B. J. Surhoff of North Carolina, both of whom were prime prospects for the major leagues, certain top draft choices.

I could've been a high draft choice, too, but I made no secret of the fact that I intended to finish my four years at Auburn and play football in the fall. The NCAA allows you to be a pro in one sport and play another in college, but the rules in the Southeastern Conference were stricter: If you're a pro in one sport, you can't play any college sports. I told everybody not to draft me, but the California Angels did anyway, in the twentieth round. They tried to get me to consider baseball, and I promised them I would—in a year.

I couldn't wait for my final college football season to start. Coach Dye told me he had decided to switch from the wishbone to the I-formation, which meant that I would be at tailback and running with the ball a lot more. He said the I-formation would give him an extra receiver and open up the passing game, but even though we never talked about it, I'm pretty sure one of the main reasons he went to the I-formation was that it would give me a better chance to win the Heisman Trophy. Coach Dye knew that the Heisman Trophy would not only be good for me, it would be good for Auburn, too.

The Auburn sports information office didn't go crazy trying to promote me for the Heisman, but there were a few stunts. When I had to pose for the *Atlanta*

Journal coming out of a phone booth, dressed like Superman, I felt like a dork. A bunch of guys working across the street couldn't stop laughing. I always liked to be inconspicuous on campus. Not on the field. In our opening game, against Southwestern Louisiana, playing out of the I-formation, I ran for 161 yards and three touchdowns—and that was just in the first quarter. I took it easy the rest of the game, but still ended up with 290 yards rushing and four touchdowns, both highs for my college career.

I got a lot of attention that week—phone calls and letters from everywhere. One of the calls came from a woman in Oxford, Alabama. She was a dietician, and she told me about a young boy she was treating, a teenager named Jon Greenwood who had lost a leg when a station wagon collided with the bicycle he was riding. I called Jon on the phone, convinced him that it really was Bo Jackson who was calling. He sounded like a good kid, but he was obviously depressed. I told him to keep his chin up.

The day before our second game, against Southern Mississippi, I decided to drive the two hours over to Oxford to see Jon, maybe to cheer him up, motivate him a little. I brought him an Auburn jersey and a banner, and we had a good visit, and then I drove back to Auburn in time for practice.

I just felt I had to go see him. Not for my schoolwork. Not even for him. I had to do it for *me*. I can't go see every kid who's sick, or every kid who needs encouragement, but whenever I can, I'm going to make time for kids. I feel I can give them something that I wish someone had given me.

I used to talk at the Pepperell Elementary School in Opelika, tell the kids that people who use drugs are crazy and people who use alcohol are crazy, and I used to speak at the Helen Keller School for the Blind and Deaf in Talladega, tell them about what I went through as a child. I also visited the Girls' and Boys' Ranch in Auburn, a home for children who had been sexually abused. The kids needed someone to teach them right from wrong, but more important they needed someone who cared. I don't know how much I accomplished, but I cared.

The day after I saw Jon Greenwood, I ran for more than 200 yards againt Southern Miss and scored two touchdowns. In our first six games, I averaged more than 200 yards rushing a game, averaged two touchdowns a game and had a pair of 76-yard runs. The only game in which I failed to score, the only game in which I didn't gain even 100 yards, was the Tennessee game, which was our only defeat in the first six games.

I strained my knee in the third quarter against Tennessee, and I remembered the Texas game from the year before, when I kept playing after I banged up my shoulder. If you play hurt, you get hurt worse. I took myself out of the game. I let the coaches know my knee was hurting. I was healthy for our next game.

Then, in our seventh game of the season, against Florida, I bruised my thigh in the second quarter, bruised it bad enough to cause internal bleeding. I sat out almost all the rest of the game. I tried to carry the ball once in the fourth quarter, but I was just hurting the team and hurting myself.

The following week, the thigh was still bothering me, so after we built a good lead in the first half against East Carolina, I sat out the second half. I took a lot of crap for going out of three games.

The most ignorant comments were in *Sports Illustrated*, the kind of cheap shots you'd get kicked out of the game for—if you were a player. Just to get a few laughs, the writer made it sound like I was a coward who couldn't stand pain and didn't care about winning. He was the worst asshole, but he wasn't the only one. There were other writers and some fans, too, who questioned my courage, though I don't recall any of them who stood up and did it to my face.

Ninety percent of the people who attacked me never played football themselves, wouldn't even know how to hold a football. They were just showing their stupidity. I'll play banged up, I'll play in pain, but I'm not going to play to the point where I get permanently damaged—no way.

When it's all said and done, when I'm sitting home, and limping, my knee torn up at the age of twenty-three, these sportswriters and these fans are still going to be up in the stands, ripping someone else. I know what my body can do and what my body can't do—I know better than anyone else—and I'm not going to go out and force my body to do some superhuman thing just to please a sportswriter.

After East Carolina, we played Georgia, and I gained more than 100 yards in the first half—67 of them on a touchdown run that may have been the one play that clinched the Heisman Trophy for me. I didn't do much in the second half. I played the last two quarters with two cracked ribs.

I knew I had cracked ribs, and Coach Dye knew I had cracked ribs, but there was no way I was going to sit out the last game of the regular season, my last game against Alabama. The ribs were going to hurt, I knew that, but they weren't going to get any worse. They were still going to be cracked at the end of the game.

The cracked ribs were bad enough, but a few days before the game, Tommie Agee and Tim Jessie and I decided to go horseback riding. It wasn't a very smart thing to do. Tommie's horse backed into mine and then kicked me in the left shin. It hurt like hell. I went and had it checked out, quietly, and found out I had a hairline fracture. I didn't even tell Coach Dye. He might've killed me.

I played the whole game against Alabama. I carried the ball thirty-one times, against guys who would've been happy to crack every bone in my body. I gained almost 150 yards, which put me over 4,300 for my career, an Auburn record, and I scored our first two touchdowns. But we still lost. We lost on a last-second field goal, 25–23, our second loss in a row to Alabama.

I'll never forget the four games I played against the Tide, the team I'd grown up pulling for. Every game was decided by one, two or three points: 23–22, 23–20, 17–15, 25–23. In the four games, I carried the ball ninety times for six touchdowns and 630 yards, an average of 7 yards a carry. All four games were played in Birmingham, twelve miles from my home, in front of my family and my friends.

A few days after my final Alabama game, the Auburn sports information office arranged for me to meet with the media, to talk about the Heisman Trophy. The winner was going to be announced in New York that Saturday. The Heisman is the most prestigious individual award in college football.

The same day I faced the press, a group called Gifts, Inc., arranged for me to meet an eleven-year-old boy named Rusty. Gifts, Inc., granted wishes to children who were chronically or terminally ill or were the victims of child abuse. Rusty had leukemia. He was hoping to go to Seattle to have a bone marrow transplant.

Rusty's wish was to meet me. He told me he also wished that I would win the Heisman Trophy. I wished I could have taken him hunting or fishing or swimming. I wished I could have shown him how to get in trouble, doing the things kids are supposed to do. It's so sad that kids like Rusty don't get a chance to see what the world is really like. Hospitals and needles and chemotherapy and doctors and nurses—that's all they know.

Rusty helped me keep the Heisman in perspective. I wanted to win it, I wanted to win it very much, but if I didn't, I still had my health, I still had my family. There are so many things more important than honors and awards.

I guess I'd been the favorite for the Heisman, the front-runner, until my last four games, until my stats fell off. I was one of four candidates who were brought to New York to be present for the announcement of the winner. It was being done on television—live.

Two of the four finalists were quarterbacks— Chuck Long of Iowa and Vinny Testaverde of Miami. Two were tailbacks—me and Lorenzo White of Michigan State. Long and I were both seniors, and I was pretty sure that one of us was going to be the winner.

We sat together, the four finalists, waiting to hear who'd won. The president of the Downtown Athletic Club, which presents the Heisman Trophy, stood up and said, "It's a pleasure to announce the winner of this year's Heisman Memorial Trophy. In the closest vote in the history of this trophy . . ."

He paused. For about three days. I wasn't nervous—until then. It seemed like an eternity. My heart

Spud and Nick have a million toys, but, more important, they have a mother *and* a father.

© 1989 Wakefield's of Kansas City, Inc.

My only surviving high school photo. Courtesy Florence Jackson Bond

Coach Pat Dye brought me to Auburn, and Lionel (The Little Train) James showed me around.

Courtesy Auburn University

The Little Train and I took turns blocking for each other and cheering for each other.

Courtesy Auburn University

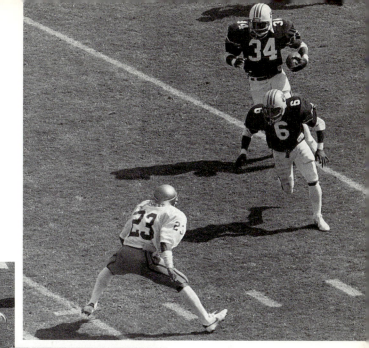

I played football and baseball at Auburn, and everyone said I'd have to pick one or the other when I turned pro. Everyone was wrong.

Courtesy Auburn University

I lived by my own Golden Rule at Auburn: "It is better to give a lick than to receive one." If anybody got in my way, I tried to run right through him.

Courtesy Auburn University

When we marched into New Orleans for The Sugar Bowl, Bo knew music—and Bo knew hats.

Courtesy Auburn University

When I broke free against Georgia my senior year, I went 67 yards for the touchdown that may have clinched the Heisman Trophy.

Courtesy Auburn University

When I was a freshman, I decided I was going to win the Heisman Trophy. When I was a senior, I said the thought had never even crossed my mind. Photo by Chuck Benson

started pounding so hard I thought everyone in the room could hear it.

". . . Bo Jackson of Auburn."

I stood up, shook hands with the other players and accepted the trophy. Then I called my mom. Everybody in the neighborhood was at her house, all my family, all my friends. They were having a party. I could hear the caps coming off the beer bottles. The party lasted through the night.

I stayed over in New York till Monday, and then when I flew back to Auburn, I couldn't believe the crowd that was waiting for me outside Sewell Hall, the band playing, thousands of people cheering, standing on cars, waving banners, demanding that I give a speech. It was the most exciting moment of my four years at Auburn. "It's nice to get away from New York," I told the crowd. "It's too fast for me."

Linda sent me roses, and like a dumb ass, instead of going to celebrate with her, I went out with my buddies. You name it, and I drank it that night. I'm glad all the kids I used to give talks to didn't see me. I was so drunk I passed out on the floor of a buddy's place. When I woke up in the morning, I was sick as a dog. That was the last time in my life I was drunk.

I recovered in time to go back to New York a few days later for the Heisman dinner. I aimed my acceptance speech at young people. "Set your goals high," I told them, "and don't stop till you get there." I was wearing a tuxedo for the first time in my life, and I was in a room full of people wearing tuxedos, and I was scared. But I took my time and, even if I stuttered a little, I said what I wanted to say.

A few weeks later, we lost to Texas A&M in the Cotton Bowl, the only bowl game we lost during my four college years. Then I played in the Japan Bowl, had a ball in Tokyo, my first and, so far, only trip overseas. The next week was the Senior Bowl, another all-star game, and they wanted me to fly from Japan to Los Angeles to Atlanta to Mobile and go right to practice.

"No, I'm going home," I said. "If I can't take a day or two to get over this jet lag, I won't play."

I went home, then drove to Mobile. In the game, I broke away and somebody ran me down and caught me from behind, I was so tired.

Everywhere I went, people wanted to know whether I was going to play pofessional football or professional baseball. I told them the truth. I told them I didn't know. I told them I wasn't going to make up my mind until June, until I had finished my senior year at Auburn. "Money isn't the main thing," I kept saying. "Money can't buy happiness, and Bo Jackson wants to be happy." I told them the truth, and nobody believed me.

In February, I started getting ready for my senior baseball season. I was really looking forward to it. We had a strong team, a powerful lineup. I got off to a slow start—I was batting only .246 through twenty games—but I was leading the team with seven home runs.

Then I got in trouble.

The trouble started with a friend—I *thought* he was a friend—who was acting as sort of an adviser to me. Not an agent, a family adviser. When I was a teenager, I used to cut his lawn, and he used to pay me and give me little gifts: a pair of cowboy boots, a stereo, a shotgun. He didn't ask for anything in return. Then later, when I was in college, he said, "You ought to think about letting me act as your agent." I didn't want to hurt him, I didn't want to say no, so I just said, "I'll think about it."

All he was thinking about was him. He was just out for one thing: to make money for himself. He tried to make a fool out of me.

There are plenty of vultures who are looking to take advantage of athletes. Some of them are white, and some are black. Most of the athletes who get taken advantage of are black. Maybe 95 percent of us grew up with nothing, and so, when somebody says to us, "Hey, here's five hundred, here's a thousand to hold you over, let me know if you need more and, oh yeah, when you're ready to turn pro, I'll get you the best deal," we get sucked in, too many of us. They con you and they fool you, and they get you locked in.

It's bad enough when it's white guys taking advantage of black athletes, but to me, it's even worse when black guys do it:

"You should let a brother handle your business."

"Where'd you go to school, brother?"

"Well, I didn't exactly finish."

"You think I'm gonna allow somebody who didn't finish college to handle my money? Man, get a real life! Stop mooching off people."

I had that conversation more than once.

The guy I thought was my friend told a lot of people that he was my agent. He told the Tampa Bay Buccaneers that he was my agent. The Bucs had the first choice in the National Football League draft. They had the first pick because they won two games and lost fourteen in 1985, the worst record in the NFL. Tampa Bay was thinking about making me their first choice.

The NFL draft was scheduled for the end of April. In March, my so-called friend got together with the owner of the Bucs, Hugh Culverhouse, and they arranged for me to fly to Tampa Bay in Culverhouse's private jet for a physical examination. I was a little worried. I didn't want to violate any NCAA or Southeastern Conference rules. I didn't want to lose my eligibility in baseball.

My "friend" assured me that he and the Bucs had checked with the NCAA and the SEC and there was no problem. "You're just going for a physical," he said. "You're not signing anything. You're not getting any money. It's perfectly okay. Trust me."

I trusted him. I trusted the Bucs. I took the ride in Culverhouse's jet, took the physical and flew back to Auburn. A couple of days later, my baseball coach, Hal Baird, asked me about the trip. "Did you go to Tampa Bay for a physical?" he said.

"Yes, I did," I told him.

"I think they've declared you ineligible to play baseball," Coach Baird said.

That was it. My college baseball career—my college athletic career—was over. I went behind the dugout and cried.

I think I know what happened. I don't know for sure, but I suspect my "friend" made a deal with the Bucs—a you-get-Bo-to-come-down-to-Tampa-and-here's-what's-in-it-for-you deal. Then, after I made the trip, somebody—it could've been my "friend" or somebody associated with the Bucs—called the SEC and told them about it. Somebody knew it was against SEC rules. Somebody knew I'd be declared ineligible. Somebody *wanted* me to be declared ineligible. Somebody thought I'd forget about baseball—I'd *have to* forget about baseball—and Culverhouse would have me.

After I was declared ineligible, my "adviser" came to my room. "I don't want to talk to you," I told him. "I don't want to see you."

"Well, if that's the case," he said, "you have to pay me back for all the stuff I've given you."

I exploded. "Here's the boots, here's this, here's that, take it, take everything, I don't want anything that reminds me of you," I said. "Just get the hell out of here, and good riddance."

I hope I never see him again.

━━━━━

I was miserable not playing baseball. In April, not long before the NFL draft, I accepted an invitation to visit a baseball team, the California Angels. The Angels no longer had the right to sign me—that right automatically expired when I returned to Auburn for my senior year—but they were still interested in me. They wanted me to see a ball game—I had never been to a major league baseball game, or to a regular season NFL game, for that matter—and meet some of their people. They especially wanted me to meet Reggie Jackson.

I never was much at following professional sports, and when I was young, when Reggie was at his peak, I didn't know him from Adam, I just knew he was a black guy who played for the Yankees and his last name was Jackson. Because of his last name, I used to tell kids that he was my cousin.

Reggie wasn't my hero. I only had two heroes in my life: my mom and Chuck Yeager. If I had gone into the military, instead of going into professional sports, I would've become a test pilot. I would've become a black Chuck Yeager.

When I met Reggie Jackson in the spring of 1986, he told me that I was in a great position. "You can play football and be the next Jim Brown," he said, "or you can play baseball and be the next Reggie Jackson."

I thought maybe he was trying to be funny. He wasn't. A few years later, when I was with the Royals and he was in the last season of his career, he said to me, "Baseball's been good to me, but I've been *great* to baseball." He was serious. I just walked away. I was kind of sorry we had the same last name.

Everyone kept pressing me—football or baseball? Tampa Bay or the minor leagues?—and I told everyone I didn't like buses, didn't like buses since I had to ride one to junior high, and I knew that you had to ride buses in baseball's minor leagues. But I also told everyone that I loved baseball, and I loved football, each in its own season, and I wasn't going to make my decision before June. When I say something, believe it.

I knew I needed someone to represent me. I wanted someone who was smart and honest, someone I could trust. I went to the Auburn trustee who was the president of the Colonial Bank in Birmingham and I asked him for his advice. I respected his experience and his judgment. He recommended a law firm in Mobile. Richard Woods and Tommy Zieman worked for that firm. By the middle of April 1986, they were my lawyers.

━━━━━━

I was lucky. With the right help, I picked the right people. Tommy Zieman represented me just in the spring of 1986, but Richard Woods is still my lawyer. He went to Wesleyan University and to Alabama Law School. I respect his intelligence, and his opinions, and he respects mine. Susann McKee works for Richard. I've known her since I was a freshman at Auburn; her daughter was a friend of mine. Richard does all the legal work; Susann does a lot of the legwork. If I shoot a commercial, she's usually there; if I appear on a TV show, she's usually there. She's always reminding me of what I have to do, and where I have to be, and when. She stays in touch with Linda and with my mom, too. Susann cares about me, and so does Richard. They care about my kids, too.

━━━━━━

My lawyers immediately made it clear to Tampa Bay—to Hugh Culverhouse—that I was seriously considering baseball as a career. Culverhouse didn't believe it. He said he'd talked with people in baseball and they'd told him I didn't have the talent. I don't know who he talked to. Maybe George Steinbrenner. Steinbrenner lives in Tampa. Maybe they're neighbors. (I'm thinking of building my permanent home in Florida, but I don't think I'll live in *that* neighborhood.)

Several NFL teams tried to persuade Tampa Bay to trade their number one choice. The San Francisco 49ers were one of them. Before the NFL draft, I flew out to California, talked to a few baseball teams and talked to Bill Walsh, who was then the coach and general manager of the 49ers. I liked Walsh. "I'd love to play for you," I told him. Walsh tried to make a deal with Culverhouse—I heard he offered a package of players and draft choices, a good package—but Culverhouse said no.

If the 49ers had made the trade, if they had been able to draft me, I probably would've gone right into football. I probably wouldn't have been able to resist. San Francisco is a special organization—they treat their players with respect—and by now, I'd have at least two Super Bowl rings, and maybe more.

Culverhouse turned everybody down. He had made up his mind. He was going to choose first, and he was going to choose me.

I wasn't happy about it. I didn't want to play for him. I didn't like what the Bucs had done to me, costing me my senior baseball season, and I didn't like Culverhouse's attitude toward me. And I really didn't want to play for a team as bad as Tampa Bay. I'd seen their offensive line. I didn't want to get beat up every week.

My lawyers started talking money, and Tampa Bay's first offer was insulting. "Tell Culverhouse I'm going to be the first player picked in the first round of the draft," I said to Richard, "and I think I should name my own price."

The Bucs came back with another offer, which wasn't much better than the first. "If you don't take this by Monday," they said, "we're going to cut it in half."

I told Richard and Tommy to tell them to go fuck themselves. "I won't play for Culverhouse," I said. "Unless he trades me, I'm not going to play football, not as long as Tampa Bay has the rights to me. When my name goes back in the draft, then I'll think about football again."

I suppose Tampa Bay could've made me an offer that I couldn't turn down, but I was still hoping they'd trade me. (I never *demanded* that they trade me; I didn't think that would do me any good.) The Bucs acted as if they still thought I'd come running to them. They figured the USFL was dead, and they were the only game in town. The only football game.

My lawyers kept looking into baseball. They checked, directly or indirectly, with guys like Kirk Gibson and Rick Leach and Steve Bartkowski, guys who'd had a choice of football or baseball, and almost to a man they said they were glad they chose baseball or wish they had. But of course none of them had won the Heisman Trophy.

Richard Woods talked to a lot of baseball teams, and I went to meet some of them, Kansas City and Toronto, for instance. The hard part was convincing people that I really was thinking about playing baseball. Everyone knew I could make more money right away by playing football, but if quick money was all I cared about, I would've signed with the Yankees in high school. I knew—and my advisers knew—that baseball, with a much higher pay scale and longer careers, could be more profitable in the long run. *If*— if I had big league talent. There never was any *if* in my mind.

When I went to visit Toronto, one of the Blue Jays' outfielders, Lloyd Moseby, saw me in the clubhouse and said, "I hear you're supposed to be pretty fast."

I kind of looked at him and nodded, and he reached into his locker and pulled out a stack of money, a thick stack—I don't know how much—and said, "I'll bet you I can beat you."

I didn't have any money, but no way I was going to back down. "Okay," I said. "You wear your cleats, and I'll wear my street shoes."

Moseby looked at me like I was crazy, then put his money back in his locker. He shook his head. "I'm not running against nobody that cocky," he said.

A few baseball teams said that if I would commit myself to baseball, they would pick me in the first round of the draft. They said they really couldn't talk money up front, but one general manager said he'd pay me $4 million for four years if I gave him my word I'd choose baseball.

I told him what I told everyone, that the size of the offer wouldn't be the determining factor. What was important was what was going to make Bo Jackson happy. I don't think anybody really believed me.

At the end of May, a month after the football draft and a few days before the baseball draft, I went off to the Caribbean to do some scuba diving. I had no phone, no television, nothing to do but dive down more than a hundred feet and stare at sharks and barracudas. It was a lot like negotiating with Tampa Bay.

A few days after I returned to Auburn, the Kansas City Royals selected me in the fourth round of the baseball draft. I was glad it was Kansas City. Of the baseball teams I'd visited, I'd been most impressed by the Royals. The world champion Royals.

Richard and I went to Memphis, the hometown of the new co-owner of the Royals, Avron Fogelman. Like most people in baseball, Mr. Fogelman thought I was probably going to play football. I was a known quantity in football; I was a question mark to some people in baseball. I told Mr. Fogelman I really hadn't made up my mind, I wanted to hear his best offer. Then I'd decide what was right for Bo Jackson.

Kansas City made its proposal, Tampa Bay made its proposal—and the offers came down to this:

If I chose Tampa Bay and football, I would be guaranteed $2 million—and I would probably earn more than $4 million in the next five years.

If I chose Kansas City and baseball, I would be guaranteed $200,000—and I would probably earn no more than $1 million in the next three years.

In addition, Nike wanted to sign me to an endorsement contract, and they offered to pay me several times more if I chose football than if I chose baseball.

On the basis of dollars and cents, I had to pick football.

Anyone would pick football.

I picked baseball.

Why? For a variety of simple reasons. I liked batting practice. I hated football practice. I liked the idea of a long career. I hated the idea of a knee injury. I liked Avron Fogelman. I hated Hugh Culverhouse.

And, of course, I loved to surprise people.

"Now it's time for what I love to do," I announced on June 21, 1986. "It's the first day of summer. Let's play ball!"

I never said I didn't love football, too.

The waitress came to his table and discreetly handed Bo Jackson a folded note. She nodded toward a group of women sitting at a table in the corner, secretaries perhaps, or executives, on their lunch hour in the suburbs of Kansas City. Bo unfolded the note. "We know you don't give autographs," he read, "so we're going to give you our autographs."

Bo looked at the women's signatures. "I don't know where they got the idea I don't give autographs," he said.

They might have gotten the idea from the dark look that usually flashes across Bo Jackson's face when he is asked for an autograph. The look is intimidating, which is not necessarily Bo's intention. He is capable of making "Hello" seem intimidating.

The truth is that Bo Jackson, like a large percentage of the people who are regularly called upon to sign autographs (which includes politicians, entertainers and athletes, the three branches of show business), does not relish the experience, finds it often intrusive and occasionally insulting.

But because a part of him recognizes a vague obligation to the people who buy the products that pay his salaries, and another part of him recognizes a more substantial responsibility to offer youngsters a role model, and because his wife urges him to be at least polite to his admirers, Bo does sign autographs.

Sometimes.

"I can feel the stares, the whispers, when I walk in," Bo said. "There's ten or twelve people wondering should they ask or shouldn't they, and once one comes, they all come."

A man sitting at the next table leaned toward Bo, reached out and proffered a sheet of paper. "I hate to bother you," the man said, "but . . ."

"Just leave it," Bo said.

The man dropped the sheet of paper on Bo's table.

Bo picked up the menu and studied the standard fare: nachos, potato skins, chicken wings, burgers.

"I'll sign in public when people are discreet about it," he said. "Don't yell my name out real loud. Don't shout across the room. Don't attract attention. Don't demand, 'Sign this.' Be polite.

"Don't send a two-year-old up to ask for my autograph. 'My daddy told me to come over . . .' He doesn't have any idea who I am. That's insulting me—and your child."

Bo ordered frogs' legs. He always does the unexpected. He picked up the piece of paper the man had left on his table, signed it and asked the waitress to return it.

"The proper time is at the ballpark," he said. "I set aside time at the park. Those are business hours. But don't call my hotel room and ask can I come downstairs. And don't walk up to me while I'm eating. Don't expect me to put my fork down and let my food get cold. Don't invade my privacy."

Bo has a sign bolted to the front door of his home which expresses his philosophy: ABSOLUTELY NO AUTOGRAPHS. THANK YOU. He is at the opposite end of the celebrity spectrum from Muhammad Ali, who, during his youthful championship days, used to invite the sightseers who drove by his Cherry Hill, New Jersey, home to come inside and see the rooms and meet the family.

"I will not sign autographs when I'm with my wife and kids," Bo said. "I won't cheat my family. Some people understand. They say, 'I see where you're coming from.' Some people get mad. They say, 'That asshole, he wouldn't give me an autograph.' That doesn't bother me. I've been called worse."

The waitress brought Bo his frogs' legs.

"I only asked for an autograph once in my life," he said, "and that wasn't for me. I was going on the Oprah Winfrey show a couple of years ago, and one of my teammates, Frank White, asked me if I would get Oprah's autograph for his son, and I did."

Bo took the note from the women at the corner table, and on the bottom wrote them a note explaining that he does sign autographs, signed his name and, discreetly, called over the waitress and asked her to deliver it for him.

"The only autograph I would ask for," Bo said, "is Chuck Yeager's. I'd love to meet him. I'd like to go fishing with him for half a day, then go up in a jet with him."

Bo sounded just like a fan. "I could die after that," he said. "I wouldn't care."

4

I SIGNED A LIFETIME CONTRACT—WITH LINDA

Many of the reporters at my news conference in Birmingham were surprised that I had chosen baseball. Some of them were skeptical. They mentioned my batting average in my final season at Auburn and wondered if I could play baseball. "Let me state a fact," I told them. "Bo Jackson can play baseball."

I wasn't bragging. I was just stating a fact. I'd been playing baseball since I was ten years old, and if I couldn't play, I would've known it by then. I know what I can do, and what I can't do.

I was glad to be going to work, glad to be earning a living. I wasn't going to be just hanging out, in Bessemer, or in Auburn. I had bought myself a new car, a black Alfa. In four years, I had stepped up from a '67 Riviera to an '86 Alfa.

After the news conference, my mom, Richard Woods, Susann McKee and I got on board Avron Fogelman's private jet and flew with him to Kansas City. The Royals wanted me to spend a few days with the big league team, get my batting eye—I hadn't played a baseball game in more than two months, hadn't even taken batting practice—and then report to the Memphis Chicks, Kansas City's Double-A farm team in the Southern League.

The Royals were a good team. They had won the World Series in 1985. They had George Brett and Willie Wilson and Bret Saberhagen and Frank White. I was looking forward to joining them.

I felt great, considering I'd been up all night, the night before, saying goodbye to my friends. And I wasn't nervous. I didn't have time to be nervous. But I did show up at the ballpark without my shoes, my glove or my bat. I left them on Mr. Fogelman's plane.

I borrowed a pair of spikes, and a glove, and then, when I went out on the field, I borrowed a bat from Steve Balboni, who was a few inches taller than me and several pounds heavier. His bat was longer and heavier than I was accustomed to—thirty-five inches, thirty-five ounces. I was used to using a thirty-three- or thirty-four-inch bat, thirty-one or thirty-two ounces.

I took my turn in the batting cage, fouled off a few, hit a few grounders, then hit one ball pretty solid, to straightaway center field, over the fence, on the fly to the base of the scoreboard, which is shaped like a crown and is more than 450 feet from home plate. You should have seen the look on Mr. Fogelman's face. He was like a kid with a new toy. He asked if he could keep the ball. He was more excited than I was. It was just batting practice.

A couple of the guys on the team told me their kids had watched me play football on television and would love to have a photograph of me with the Heisman Trophy. Did I have any? I said no, but I'd get some. I called Auburn and asked the people in the athletic department to send me a couple of dozen photos. When they arrived, a day or two later, I gave them to the guys who had asked for them and left the rest in my locker.

The word got around that I had just waltzed in, the cocky college kid, and begun handing out pictures of myself. It wasn't quite that way.

George Brett asked me for one of the pictures and put it up over his locker. He wasn't making fun of me. He said he wished he could've won the Heisman Trophy. George was probably the friendliest of all the guys on the team. Maybe because he was the best player, the most secure. He gave me one of his bats to take with me to Memphis. It came in handy, though not the way George expected.

Memphis was a zoo. Reporters and cameras everywhere I turned, and a general manager who drove me crazy. He had me come in to sign things for three thousand of his friends. Balls. Photographs. I did it. I didn't want to be difficult; I didn't want to get on his bad side, but he was a pain.

I played my first professional game on June 30, 1986, and more than seven thousand fans, more than twice as many as usual, showed up to watch. I was the designated hitter—they wanted me to polish up my fielding before they put me in the outfield in a game— and my first time at bat, in the bottom of the first inning, I got a single that drove in a run. They asked me if I wanted the ball to keep. I said no. It was just a ground ball up the middle.

I didn't get another base hit that night, or the next, or the next. I was one for eleven as a designated hitter. Then I went into the outfield. I was two for thirty-one with fourteen strikeouts. Then I was four for forty-five. I was batting under .100 after two weeks of professional baseball. One of the pitchers who struck me out said I was overmatched in the Southern League.

I liked hearing that. I liked hearing that I wasn't good enough, that I couldn't do something. I wasn't worried. I really wasn't. I knew everybody was expecting too much right away. People wanted me to be Superman. I was feeling the pressure. "Relax," I thought. "Just be yourself. Do what you can do."

On July 13, 1986, back at Auburn, Linda gave birth to Garrett. I couldn't get there to see him right away, but I sent Tommie Agee and Tim Jessie to see him and Linda, and they told me he was a winner. Then I started to hit. One week in July, I went eleven for twenty-six with three triples and three home runs. I hit one home run in Memphis—score tied, bottom of the ninth, bases loaded—that sailed out of the baseball stadium and into the football stadium next door. They said it was the longest home run in the history of the Southern League. The manager of the other team said the ball must've traveled 600 feet. I don't think so. Maybe 550, 560.

The general manager at Memphis wouldn't leave me alone, kept taking advantage of me. It wasn't bad enough he was always asking me for autographs—and I was signing them for the fans every night—he also asked me if I would sit down for thirty minutes and do an interview with a friend of his son's. His son was in high school. So was his son's friend. He wanted to interview me for the school paper. "No," I said, "I can't do that. I don't even have time for *USA Today*. I can't do it."

He brought the kid to the locker room anyway, brought him right up to my locker and asked me again to do the interview. I turned to the kid and said. "Look, I told him ten times I couldn't do this, but he insisted on bringing you here, embarrassing me and embarrassing you. I apologize, but I do not have time to do an interview with you." When the kid left, I ripped the general manager up and down, cussed him out, threatened him, everything. He was terrified. I think he thought I was going to hit him.

Our manager was laughing his ass off in his office and our coaches were rolling on the floor. Once the general manager backed out of the locker room, the players were rolling on the floor, too. They said they were wondering how long I was going to take his crap. They were waiting for me to explode.

Life in the Southern League was not glamorous. The buses were bigger and nicer than the ones that used to take me to junior high, but the rides were a lot longer. Twelve hours from Memphis to Greenville, South Carolina. A typical Southern League trip. I liked the guys I was playing ball with. They got on me a lot. Some of them even wore Tampa Bay football jerseys. Most of them were young kids, just out of high school, or a year or two of college, young and crazy.

The two I was closest to were my age, or a little older: Mike Miller, who played second base and shortstop, and Jere Longenecker, who played first base. We used to go out to eat together, and they'd walk into the restaurant and call out, "Hey, hey, hey, we're hungry, and Bo is paying. We're just minor leaguers, and he's got a big league contract." It was good-natured, and I always paid; I didn't mind. Mike and Jere never made it to the majors. They're both out of baseball now, Mike's in Minnesota and Jere's in Connecticut, both of them married, and I'm still in touch with them. When Mike got married, I gave him a special wedding present. I sent him and his wife to Bermuda for a week for their honeymoon.

I had one ugly experience in Memphis. Susann McKee, from Richard Woods's office, came in from Mobile to go over some business things with me. She came to a game, and afterward we were walking through a parking lot to my black Alfa, and I heard somebody yell at Susann, "Nigger lover!"

I looked around, didn't see anybody, walked Susann to my car, then looked around again. Finally I made out four guys sitting in a station wagon. I walked over to them. "Any of you say that?" I said.

They were young guys. They all shook their heads.

I walked back to my car. Halfway there, I heard laughter coming from the station wagon.

I went to my car, opened the trunk and took out the bat that George Brett had given me. I walked to the station wagon. The windows were now closed. "Open the windows," I said, "or I'll smash in every one of them."

The driver opened his window, and I stuck the bat in his face.

"I'm not a violent person," I said, "but this bat has George Brett's name on it, and if someone doesn't apologize fast, you're going to have George Brett's name on your forehead."

The driver apologized. I said, "Thank you," and went back to my car.

The next day, the four men complained to the Memphis club that they were season ticket holders and they had been harassed in the parking lot by one of the ballplayers. The club looked into the incident—and I was told they took away the men's season tickets, barred them from the ballpark.

I wasn't unhappy to leave Memphis after two months. I had batted .338 after my slow start, and I was going up to spend the final month of the 1986 season with the Kansas City Royals.

But before I reported, I drove home and went to see Linda and Garrett. He was six weeks old, and I fell in love with him at first sight. I hated to leave him so quickly, but I had to play baseball.

On September 2, I played my first major league game, in Kansas City, against the Chicago White Sox. Steve Carlton was pitching for the White Sox. I didn't know who he was; I didn't know who any of the pitchers were. I didn't follow sports. I had no idea Carlton had won more than 300 games. I didn't even know he was left-handed till I saw him pitch in the first inning.

My first time up, in the second inning—I was sixth in the batting order—Carlton threw me a hanging curve, and I hammered it, hit it over the foul pole, up by the concession stands in left field. It was a drive. By the time the ball landed, I was already at second base. The umpire called it foul. I came that close to hitting a home run in my first time at bat in the big leagues.

I stepped back in and hit a high hopper between first and second. The first baseman went over and fielded the ball, and I beat Carlton to the bag and had my first hit in the major leagues. I didn't get another hit that game. Carlton shut us out.

I didn't know any more about big league pranks than I knew about big league pitchers, so when a few of the veterans pulled the old spoiled-cake trick on the rookie, I fell for it. Saberhagen had the cake in front of his locker, and a bunch of the guys stopped to look at it and smell it. Everybody had a comment.

"Man, that cake smells funny."

"Must be spoiled. Must've gone rotten."

"Hey, Bo, you smell it."

I walked over to Saberhagen's locker, leaned over to smell the cake and, just as my nose got right up to the icing, I felt Saberhagen's hand coming down hard on the back of my head. My neck stiffened. He couldn't push my face all the way down into the cake. I just got a little icing on my eyebrows. Then I scooped up a fistful of the cake and smeared it in Saberhagen's face.

Saberhagen and Mark Gubicza are the pranksters of the Royals. I wouldn't put anything past them. They love pranks. I don't. I don't like practical jokes, and when I get into a mood, I don't like being needled, either. I don't react well. I usually say something like, "Shut your mouth, or you'll get your damn teeth down your throat." Most guys understand; they shut their mouths.

In my fifth major league game, I went four for five, four infield hits, and people started saying that with my speed I ought to be a leadoff hitter. Then, a couple of days later, I hit my first big league home run—off Seattle's Mike Moore; it was supposed to be the longest in the history of Royals Stadium, about 475 feet to left-center, and people started saying that with my power I belonged in the middle of the lineup.

Top or middle, I still had a lot to learn. I batted .207 during my month with the Royals and struck out too many times. I figured I would probably have to go back to the minors in 1987, play either in Memphis again or in Triple-A ball in Omaha.

At the end of the 1986 season, the Royals asked me if I'd like to play in the Instructional League in Florida. They made it clear it was an invitation, not a command, and I said, "Sure, I'll go." I figured it would be a good learning experience.

The only good thing about the Instructional League was that I got to know Ed Napoleon, a coach and instructor who became a close friend. He worked with me on my throwing and my fielding, hit balls to me for hours, really helped me. He's with the Houston organization now, but I think of him a lot.

But the man in charge of the Instructional League camp was a little dictator who kept cussing and screaming all the time, mostly at teenagers who were terrified to death.

I lasted about two weeks, and then I decided, "I've got to go home. I can't take this. I miss Linda and Garrett too much." After a game against the Cleveland Indians' rookies, I walked into the office of the guy who was running the camp and I said, "I'm going home," and he started screaming at me, "You can't go home. Who do you think you are?"

"The Royals said it was an invitation," I said, "and I think I've overstayed my welcome. Whether you like it or not, you tell the Royals, 'Bo's going home.' " And I caught the next flight to Atlanta.

I went home first, visited with my mom and my family and my friends, then went to Auburn, back to classes and to training. It was still football season, but I didn't go to any football games. I didn't miss football.

I knew that if I ever wanted to play, I could; I still had the ability.

But I was too busy trying to establish myself as a baseball player to think about football. I was so serious about wanting to be ready to play ball in the spring that I ran two and a half miles early each morning—as much as I hate to run more than a hundred yards at a time—went to classes for a couple of hours, then worked out with the Auburn baseball team, hitting balls and shagging flies.

I also spent a lot of time with Linda and Spud. Once we were all together, I knew that the side of Bo Jackson that went around chasing women, going to bars and hitting on women, the side that was a whore, really, was over. It was time for me to settle down.

At Christmas, I went home to Bessemer with two special presents, one for my mom and one for my Aunt Bea. On Christmas morning, I handed my mom the papers for a brand-new silver custom van and handed Aunt Bea the papers for a brand-new golden yellow Cadillac. Aunt Bea had always said she wanted a Cadillac. She didn't know what the papers were. "Thank you," she said to me, "I really needed an address book."

"Address book! That's the manual, the guide to your '87 Cadillac!"

She didn't believe me till I took her outside and she saw the car that was parked there. Aunt Bea was so proud of that Cadillac.

After Christmas, Linda and Spud and I went back to Auburn, and the night before I left for spring training, in February, Linda and I were sitting at a table studying, and I reached over and handed her a little box. She opened it and saw the engagement ring I had bought for her. "I didn't think it would be right for me to go to spring training without giving you this," I said.

We got married the following September. I was only twenty-four then, but I had been around, I had been around a whole lot, and I knew I didn't want to come home to an empty apartment any more.

I think that was the smartest move I've made in my life, marrying the woman that I'm with right now. Somebody once asked me if I'd consider signing a lifetime contract with the Royals, and I said, "Hell no, I've got a lifetime contract with my wife, and that's the only lifetime contract I need."

Linda truly is the better half of Bo Jackson. She's always there for me, always warm, always comforting. I can talk to her about anything. She's my transmission. Without her, my car can't run.

There's not a day that goes by when I'm on the road that I don't talk to Linda at least twice, usually three times. I'll call her in the morning when I get up, call her in the afternoon before I go to the ballpark and call her again right after the game. I carry a cellular phone with me and sometimes I'll even call her between innings.

I don't want her to think for one moment that I'm out doing something I've got no business doing. I don't go out with the guys. I don't hang out in bars. Guys try to get me to go out with them. They say, "There's this hot new bar," and I say, "No, if I don't know what's out there, I can't miss it."

Then they'll come back and say, "Man, you missed it. It was happening last night. There were some broads looking for you, and you missed it."

I didn't miss a thing.

I like to flirt with women, smile at them, wave at them, wink at them, especially when Linda's with me, but that's all it is, just flirting. I don't think there's a woman in the world who could make me leave my family. I don't see how some guys can do it, big-name players who leave their wives and their families and run off with someone else. That's not me. I love my kids too much. I love my wife too much.

Besides, too many young people look up to me, and if they read something in the papers about Bo Jackson getting divorced, or Bo Jackson in a sex scandal, or Bo Jackson in a drug scandal, they'll probably say, "Well, Bo Jackson is just like the rest of them," and I don't want anybody to paint that image of me.

I always want to be somebody they can look up to.

I wish I'd had somebody to look up to when I was a kid.

Like so many children who were sexually abused in their own homes, the little girl did not trust people. When women approached her, she withdrew. When men approached her, she recoiled. It took Bo Jackson half a dozen visits to the Marillac Center for Children before the tiny and timid seven-year-old decided to run to him and leap onto his lap.

"It was a remarkable breakthrough," Linda Jackson said. "This child had not opened up to anyone till she met Vince."

Linda Jackson busied herself in the spacious kitchen of her suburban home, preparing spaghetti and meat sauce for her three boys: Garrett and Nicholas and Vincent.

"Children don't see him as a superstar jock," Linda said. "They see him as a person who cares about them. They don't talk about his home runs or his touchdowns. They talk about how he pushes them on the swings or holds their hands or plays catch with them."

Linda first heard about the Marillac Center in Kansas City from Eve Balboni, the wife of Bo's former teammate

Steve Balboni. With her doctoral research into the effects of sexual abuse, Linda's interest in a center that treats children for both sexual and physical abuse was logical. Inevitably, her husband became involved, too, and his involvement led to "Bat with Bo," a fund-raising campaign that encourages individuals and corporations to pledge a certain amount of money to Marillac for each home run Bo hits for the Royals. Bo's bat has already brought the center more than $100,000.

"I think athletes have an obligation to give something to the community," Linda said. "They're so fortunate that they can go and play a game they love, and get paid for it."

Linda Jackson is not the stereotypical wife of an athlete, not a grown-up cheerleader. She is a confessed bookworm who went to football games at Auburn, but didn't recognize Bo Jackson the first time she saw him without a helmet.

"But I did stare," Linda admitted. "His body does stand out."

Linda laughed. She is fiercely proud of her husband—and not only for his body. "I was surprised by how observant he was," she said, recalling the early days of their relationship. "He'd watch and study and check things out for months, and then share his observations. He didn't come to hasty decisions. I was amazed by how wise he was."

Bo and his boys came into the kitchen and sat down at the counter. Spud dove into his plate of spaghetti. Bo pushed his aside and picked up a smaller bowl and began feeding Nick. "Open your mouth," Bo commanded, and wisely Nick obeyed.

"One night we were watching television," Linda said, "and they told a story on the news about a little girl who was left on a school bus over a weekend."

"Her mother was raising her all by herself," Bo said. "She sent her to school this day, and going home the little girl fell asleep on the bus, and when the driver took the bus to the compound, he didn't have the sense to check to see if there were still any kids on board. The driver left, and when the little girl awoke—she was only about five years old—she didn't know where she was and she was afraid to get off the bus. So she just stayed where she was. And it was cold, real cold, down in the teens.

"The mother kept calling the police, trying to get them to check out the bus, but they were so slow the mother finally went herself and managed to get into the compound and found the bus and her daughter in it. The little girl had been in there freezing for more than forty-eight hours. She was frostbitten and they rushed her to the hospital and for a while the doctors didn't know if they could save her feet and her fingers."

"When they told the story on TV," Linda said, "Vince said he'd like to go see her. He got on the phone, found out what hospital she was in, went to the Children's Palace, bought a bunch of toys and went to visit her."

"I went straight up to her room," Bo said, "sat down with her and spent about thirty minutes with her. I put the batteries in her toys, talked to her, gave her a kiss on the forehead, went back downstairs and drove home."

"She didn't know who he was," Linda said, "but by the end of the visit, they were buddies."

Bo shoveled a forkful of spaghetti into Nick's mouth.

"He's just a softy at heart," Linda said.

Especially for a child without a father.

5 | EVERYBODY HAS A LITTLE JACKASS IN HIM

I like roller coasters, but only when I can sit in front, only if I can see what's coming. In 1987, I rode a roller coaster all year long, and I didn't always see what was coming. I was loved and I was hated. I was cheered and I was booed. I was a Royal and I was a Raider. In Kansas City, my name went from Bo to mud.

The year got off to a good start. In February, I had to appear at a sports show for Nike. I had to wait backstage to be introduced. I had to wait with Dale Murphy of the Atlanta Braves, Howie Long of the Los Angeles Raiders and Lawrence Taylor of the New York Giants, who had just won the Super Bowl. It was crowded backstage, all the athletes plus a bunch of models and dancers, who kept changing their outfits, pulling off their tops, boobs and asses everywhere. Howie Long, L.T. and I couldn't stop staring. Dale Murphy covered his eyes.

The year got off to a good start on the field, too. I worked hard in spring training, working with Ed Napoleon on my fielding, with Hal McRae on my hitting, concentrated on handling ground balls in the outfield, on making contact at the plate. I batted .273 in spring training, and instead of being sent to Omaha or Memphis, I stayed in Kansas City with the Royals.

Seven games into the season, I was batting .500, fourteen for twenty-eight, with three home runs and thirteen runs batted in. In one game, against Detroit, I hit two home runs and drove in seven runs, which tied the Kansas City record. Four days later, against the New York Yankees, I struck out five times in nine innings, which tied the major league record. "Boys, I stunk," I told the media.

It was that kind of year.

At the end of April, the National Football League held its annual draft. During the winter, Tampa Bay had offered to trade me—finally—to any team that I chose. The Bucs knew they were about to lose the right to negotiate with me, and before they did, they wanted to see if they could salvage something in a trade. The catch was that I would've had to commit myself to playing football, and I wasn't about to do that.

I did hear that the Indianapolis Colts were ready to pay $100,000 a year if I signed with them *even* if I didn't play; the theory was that if I ever did play, I would be under contract to them. I wasn't tempted. Robert Irsay, the man who had boasted he could sign me after my sophomore year in college, still owned the Colts.

I also heard that the Denver Broncos were interested in obtaining the rights to me, and while the idea of teaming up with John Elway did appeal to me, I didn't think about it very seriously. I knew I was a baseball player—I was batting .344 at the time of the NFL draft—and I guess the Broncos figured I was, too. They passed me up in the draft.

So did *almost* everybody else. All the NFL teams knew that I had an escape clause in my Kansas City contract, that I could buy my way out of my commitment to the Royals if I chose to give up baseball and switch to football. But Richard Woods told every NFL team that checked with him that I was happy playing baseball—and I was.

The Los Angeles Raiders didn't check with Richard. They didn't check with me. They went ahead and drafted me in the seventh round. I slipped from the #1 draft choice in 1986 to #183 in 1987.

When Richard Woods called me to tell me the Raiders had drafted me, I started singing, "California, here I come . . ." But I really didn't think it could happen. I didn't even want to think about it. I put a sign over my locker that said: DON'T BE STUPID. NO FOOTBALL QUESTIONS PLEASE. Most of the sportswriters were able to read it. Some of the television reporters, too.

I did check out the draft, looked to see how some of my former teammates did. Brent Fullwood, who did most of the ball-carrying when I was hurt my junior year, was drafted in the first round by Green Bay. Ben Tamburello, a lineman who blocked for me for three years, was picked in the third round by Philadelphia. Tommie Agee, my old roommate, was taken by Seattle in the fifth round. They all went ahead of me. Tim

Jessie went to Chicago in the eleventh round. I was rooting for all of them.

Six weeks went by after the draft without a word from the Raiders. But Al Davis, their owner, did tell some reporters that he wouldn't mind having me play football on a part-time basis, joining the Raiders after the baseball season was over. Richard Woods saw that in the paper, and when he came to Kansas City, he asked me if I'd consider playing football at the end of the baseball season.

"Is it possible?" I said.

"I don't know," Richard said. "I'll find out."

If I could've picked any team, I would've picked San Francisco. They treat their players like men, not cattle. But the Raiders would've have been my second choice. From what I'd heard, they didn't expect everybody to be the same. They let you be yourself.

The more I thought about playing football and baseball—I knew Jim Thorpe had done it a long time ago; I saw the movie about him—the more it sounded like fun. That really was the attraction: I thought it'd be fun. It had nothing to do with wanting to prove anything. I'd proved in college that I could play football. I was proving in Kansas City that I could play baseball. And it had nothing to do with money. I didn't *need* any more money than I was getting from the Royals, and I knew what it was like to live on a lot less. I just didn't want to cheat myself out of some fun. I didn't want to look back in twenty years and think, "Damn, wouldn't it have been fun doing that?"

I called Richard and said, "Hey, I'd like to play both."

"You sure?" he said.

"I'm sure."

"Well, I better call Al Davis," Richard said, "and see if he's serious."

Richard called Al Davis, and he wanted to know if *we* were serious, if I really wanted to play football, or if we were just trying to get some publicity. He wasn't sure about us, and we weren't sure about him.

Both of us were serious. Al Davis wasn't asking me to give up baseball, was perfectly willing to have me join the Raiders after the Royals' season was finished. He was also willing to sign me to a five-year contract that paid me close to $1.5 million a year and insured me against an injury that might ruin my baseball career.

Richard and Al Davis negotiated quietly, privately, for three weeks and worked it all out, but there was still one large problem. My contract with the Royals said I couldn't play football—not *and* play baseball, too. What I could do was on July 15, the "escape" date, give the Royals back all the money they had invested in me and then give up baseball and switch to football. But if I was going to stay with the Royals *and* play football—which was what I wanted to do—then we had to rewrite my contract. It was a delicate, complicated situation.

A week before July 15, the day I could exercise the escape clause, Richard Woods called Mr. Fogelman from Los Angeles and said that he would like to request permission for Bo to play football after the baseball season ended. Richard told him that I did not want to give up baseball, that the Royals were my first priority, but that I did want to play football, too, if it were possible. Mr. Fogelman was startled, but he was polite. He said he would get back to Richard.

But, instead, Mr. Fogelman got on his jet and flew to Toronto, where we were playing the Blue Jays.

He sent two messages to the ballpark, one telling Billy Gardner, our manager, to take me out of the game, and another telling me to come over to the hotel, he wanted to talk to me immediately. The manager took me out in the seventh inning, and I went into the locker room, took off my uniform and asked one of the locker room guys to clean up my locker. He cleaned *out* my locker. He took out everything, uniform, equipment, stripped it bare, packed everything up in my bag and put my bag away.

Rumors that the Raiders were negotiating with me had been going around all day, and after the game, when the players and the reporters came into the locker room and saw my locker empty, they all figured that I had quit, that I was giving up baseball, that I was gone.

My teammates didn't know what was really going on, and some of them were steaming and said some angry things. Willie Wilson said it looked like I had made fools out of them, that I had treated them like they were nothing, and Danny Tartabull said my decision would destroy the team. I don't blame them for being upset. They didn't know I was back at the hotel, talking to Mr. Fogelman, trying to explain to him that the Royals still came first with me. He was angry, too, and he was hurt, because he did care about me, and his first reaction was just to tell me to quit baseball, to pay back the Royals and to go play football.

Eventually, I got Mr. Fogelman to understand that I still considered myself a baseball player ahead of anything else. I was batting .254 at the time, with eighteen home runs and forty-five runs batted in, not great, but not bad for a rookie for half a season. Finally, he agreed to give me permission to play football. To *try* to play football, as most of the people in the Kansas City organization liked to put it. We were going to restructure my contract, to protect the Royals financially in case I got hurt playing football.

The next morning, Mr. Fogelman and I held a news conference, and I announced that I was looking into the possibility of playing professional football after the baseball season, that I was hoping to work out a contract with the Los Angeles Raiders. Mr. Fogelman said the Royals were not going to stop me from doing whatever I thought was right for Bo Jackson.

"I'm thinking about adding another hobby to my off-season curriculum," I told the reporters, "and that's all that it would be. My number one priority is the Kansas City Royals. I have to do my job with the Kansas City Royals before I do anything else. Whatever comes after the baseball season is a hobby for Bo Jackson—just like fishing and hunting."

My teammates jumped on that "hobby" line—a couple of them said they were thinking of taking up bullfighting or sharkhunting as a hobby—but once I explained to them what I was doing, and why, they understood. Each one of them had played more than one sport in his life—and knew how hard it was to give up basketball or football or whatever. George Brett said he was jealous; he always wanted to play quarterback in the NFL. Bret Saberhagen told me he would've tried it himself, except that football players were too big and too dangerous. Everybody wanted me to promise to get them tickets to the Raiders' games.

Of course some football players were a little upset by my decision, which didn't bother me at all. They didn't know me, the ones like Darryl Grant of the Redskins, who said, "I'll put a good lick on him and see how he likes his new hobby." Howie Long from the Raiders said, "It's like *One Flew Over the Cuckoo's Nest.*

Bo must've had a frontal and a rear lobotomy." I thought that was pretty funny.

What wasn't funny was the way a group of black athletes or ex-athletes attacked me on the Black Entertainment Network. They were the last people I thought would be dogging me. I thought they'd be pulling for the first black athlete to play big league baseball and big league football. Instead, they were saying, "I think this brother has bitten off more than he can chew," and "I don't think this kid knows what he's doing," and "I'll give him three or four games in the NFL, and he'll be back trying to swing a bat."

I couldn't believe it, a bunch of would-be high-society phonies sitting in their sweetwater suits, trying to play out my life for me.

Everybody ripped me in the press, too, but I expected that; I expected to bring out a little viciousness. The *Washington Post* didn't disappoint me. The headline said: ROYAL BRUISED EGO LOOKS FOR WAY OUT. The story was just as good:

> The first time Dexter Manley meets Jackson in the backfield, I'm rooting for the field mike. "Yo, Bo, let me help you put your head back on. Say, how's the hobby coming? It won't hurt your batting stroke if I tear off these two fingers, will it?"
>
> If NFL defenders have anything to say about it, Bo's new hobby will be collecting stumps . . .
>
> When Bo first showed up last season, he shook hands with the Royals before heading to Memphis in AA ball. The next week, in the mail, George Brett and others got autographed pictures of Bo in his Heisman Trophy-winning football uniform at Auburn. Brett kept the photo above his locker a long time. Too priceless to forget . . .
>
> To be a great baseball player, you need a little humility. And that, to be blunt, is why Bo Jackson is

heading for the door. If he has any significant success in cleats, you'll never see him back in spikes.

I'm told that the man who wrote all those things, Thomas Boswell, is supposed to be one of the smartest baseball writers in the business. Which tells you why, when I pick up the paper on Sundays, I keep the funnies and throw away the rest.

Right after the stormy weekend in Toronto, we took a break for the All-Star Game. I didn't go out to Los Angeles—and I didn't go back to Kansas City. I went to Auburn to see Linda and Garrett.

Linda was still in school. She and Garrett had been visiting me in Kansas City on weekends, and we were planning to get married in November, after the baseball season. But now that I was going to play football, we moved our wedding date up to September. I couldn't wait until we started living together as a family.

At a news conference in Auburn, Richard and I announced that I'd agreed to terms with the Los Angeles Raiders. I told the press that I had hired Colonel Ollie North to be my media consultant. He was getting about as good a press as I was. "He told me to answer your questions this way," I said. "I love my country, the documents have been shredded and I know nothing of this. All my actions came on orders from a higher authority."

The questions weren't much more serious. Somebody asked me how football could be a hobby if I was getting paid so much.

"It is a hobby," I said, "and I wish I could make money from fishing also."

I was asked what I thought about all the people who said I couldn't possibly succeed in two sports, that no one had ever been a professional star in both, not even Jim Thorpe. "I use that as fuel for my fire," I said, "and then I go out and prove them wrong. Every time."

I found out that one other Heisman Trophy winner, Vic Janowicz of Ohio State, had played in the NFL and in baseball's major leagues in the 1950s—and had washed out in both. I found out that a few other guys— George Halas, for instance, who ended up owning and coaching the Chicago Bears, and Tom Brown, who played for Green Bay in the first two Super Bowls—got to the majors in both football and baseball, but Jim Thorpe was the only man who lasted more than two years in both the NFL and the big leagues. And Thorpe was a Hall of Fame football player, but a journeyman baseball player.

When the All-Star break ended, I headed back to Kansas City, to play my first game in front of the hometown fans since I'd announced that I was going to play football for the Raiders. The Raiders were the most hated team in football—especially in Kansas City. They were the Kansas City Chiefs' archrivals.

I knew it was going to be rough at Royals Stadium. Almost forty thousand fans showed up for our game against Baltimore, and most of them agreed with the sign that said: BOO JACKSON. They did, the first time I came up, and threw toy footballs, dozens of them, with IT'S A HOBBY written on them. They booed even louder in the third inning when I struck out on a bad pitch. But in the fifth inning, I made a tumbling, diving catch of a line drive hit by Cal Ripken, then ended the inning with a running catch on a ball hit by Ray Knight, and when I came off the field, the fans cheered me. Many of them.

I expected the fans to boo me. I could understand

it. But I put it in my pocket. I'll never forget it. Fans are fickle. They'll boo you and call you names, and then after the game they'll beg you for your autograph.

A few days later, I made a date to go fishing with a guy I knew who had access to a backyard lake. He brought along Rick Dempsey, who was catching for Cleveland then. The Indians were in town, and this guy always offered to take visiting players fishing, too.

We caught bass in the morning and bullfrogs in the afternoon, and it got exciting when Rick caught a big bullfrog, pulled him in the boat and then, just as he reached down to grab him, a snake crawled out of the frog's mouth. The frog must've just swallowed him. The snake was about two feet long. We got him out of the boat as fast as we could.

Then that night I was on third base, and the coach said to me, "You're going home on anything hit," and the next batter hit a shot at the second baseman, and I took off, and Dempsey, being the tough and rough catcher he is, straddled home plate.

I could have hurt him real, real bad. I could have hit him in the throat and taken his head off. But since we'd been fishing that morning, and I liked him, I held back a little. Dempsey had the glove right in front of his crotch, and I decided just to hit the glove, to jar the ball loose. I didn't hold back enough. I snapped his thumb back, broke his thumb, knocked him off the plate, almost to our dugout. I was surprised. I didn't think I hit him that hard.

Most catchers don't straddle the plate against me. They give me a corner of the plate so that I can either slide by them or run by them. I never intentionally try to run over someone to hurt him. But I do like to scare him.

The rest of the 1987 baseball season was pretty much of a nightmare. Some of the people in the front office of the Royals treated me worse than the fans treated me. They acted as if I had pissed in their waterfall. Maybe they believed the stories that once I picked up a football, I'd never come back to baseball. Maybe they were jealous. I don't know. I told them that baseball was number one. I told them the truth. They should have believed me.

I didn't hit very well after the All-Star break, and every time I went into a slump, almost every time I went hitless, they pulled me out of the lineup, kept me out for two days, three days, a week, didn't let me work my way out of the slump. I heard all the whispers: "Bo's mind's on football. Bo's not thinking about baseball. Bo doesn't care. Bo's not trying." It was bullshit. They were trying to play games with my head. They were trying to hurt me. But you can't hurt a man who's been hurting all his life. My tolerance for pain is so high there is no more hurt. The girders in Royals Stadium could collapse and fall before they'd be able to get to me mentally.

One of our outfielders, Thad Bosley, asked me how to bench-press properly, and as much as I hate to lift weights, I said, "C'mon, I'll show you," and went into the weight room with him. I was in there maybe thirty seconds, and one of the coaches spotted us and went running to the manager, saying, "Bo's lifting weights, Bo's trying to get ready for football, Bo doesn't care about baseball any more."

And the next day they moved all the weights into

the training room so the trainer could keep an eye on who was using them and let the manager know. I blew up. I went in and told them, "The weights you got wouldn't help a girls' gymnastics team. If I was going to lift weights, I'd get real ones, not that stuff you've got."

I was so pissed. I was pissed the rest of the summer. They just didn't believe me. They didn't believe I could do—I *would* do—exactly what I said I was going to do, play football for the fun of it, then come back and play baseball as well as I possibly could. If anything, the fact that I was going to play football made it more important to me that I play baseball well.

After the All-Star break, I only played about half the games. I didn't even hit .200. I ended up with twenty-two home runs for the season, which was a record for Kansas City rookies, but I also ended up with 158 strikeouts, which was another record for Kansas City rookies. In September, a rookie named Gary Thurman took over in left field. They acted like he was Babe Ruth.

The only good thing that happened the last couple of months of the baseball season was that Linda and I got married on September 5, 1987, in a church in Kansas City. Now Garrett officially had a mother *and* a father to raise him.

Just as the baseball season was coming to an end, the football season suddenly stopped. The players went out on strike. The Royals invited me to go to the Instructional League again, but even if the football season was canceled, I wasn't going back to the little dictator.

Then, on the last day of the baseball season, the

football season started up again—with replacement players on all the NFL teams. It was a good break for my friend Tim Jessie, who'd played with me at Auburn. Tim had been cut by the Bears just before the season began, but during the strike he caught on with the Washington Redskins and stayed with them and wound up the year with a Super Bowl ring.

(Tim plays up in Canada now. I hear he's a star, but Tommie, Lionel and I don't see much of him. We're all married, and he's chasing French girls.)

My contract with the Raiders said that I didn't have to report till ten days after the baseball season ended. I insisted upon ten days not because I thought I needed to rest my body, or my mind, but because I wanted to make sure I had some time to spend with my family, time to get them resettled.

But ten days after the 1987 baseball season ended, the regular football players were still on strike, and I wasn't about to cross the picket line. So I got an extra week with my family before the strike was settled, and I joined the Los Angeles Raiders.

The first thing I had to do was take a physical. I hated that. I hated when they took blood. I'm afraid of needles. They hurt. I got light-headed once when a nurse just pricked my finger. I had to lie down. I'm serious. It terrifies me.

I managed to survive the physical, met the coaches, collected my gear and ran into a few players I knew from college, guys I'd played against and guys I'd played with in all-star games—and even one of my Auburn teammates, Chris Woods, a wide receiver from Birmingham. I heard that as soon as I arrived, somebody ran up to Marcus Allen, the Raiders' number one running back, and announced, "Flight 34 has landed," and Marcus knew what he meant, knew that my uniform number was 34 and knew that I'd probably be getting some of his playing time.

There had to be some resentment on his part. Marcus was used to being the man, being in the spotlight. He was a great player—a Heisman Trophy winner, too—and he'd had a great pro career. He'd led the Raiders to victory in the Super Bowl in 1984. If the situation had been reversed, I know I'd have felt some resentment.

But Marcus and I got along fine when we were together. I really do respect his ability, and I think he respects mine, and in public, we both said the right things. I don't know what he said in private. I do know that some of his friends made cracks later. After I'd been with the Raiders a couple of years, Ronnie Lott of the 49ers, who played with Marcus in college, said something like, "Well, with all the money the Raiders are paying Bo Jackson, he ought to lead them to a Super Bowl."

If there was any resentment among the other guys on the Raiders, about baseball or about my salary, it seemed to disappear pretty quick. As soon as I took a pitchout in practice and outran everybody, I could tell the guys accepted me. I knew I could still move—and they knew I could play.

I didn't have much trouble getting into the football routine. The worst part is that it's boring. You only get to play one game a week, and it's hard to get excited about practice. The best part of practice in the pros is that you don't get hit. Nobody tackles running backs or quarterbacks or wide receivers, and hardly anybody even touches you. You don't get hit until Sunday.

The meetings are worse than the workouts. The lectures and the films are *really* boring. The first week, I stayed awake most of the time, but I knew that once I got the hang of it, I'd be moving to the back of the room, leaning against the wall and going to sleep as soon as the lights went out.

I'm not putting football down. I love the game—the *games*—just as much as I love baseball, almost as much as I love hunting and fishing. I have tremendous respect for both football and baseball and for the people who have the talent to play them well. The thing is, I love to compete, I love to win and I love what I call the sports life: You can be with your buddies, you can get as dirty as you want and, in fact, the dirtier you get, the better it feels. And once in a while, you can knock the hell out of somebody and you don't have to worry about getting punished for it.

But baseball and football are very different games. In a way, both of them are easy. Football is easy if you're crazy as hell. Baseball is easy if you've got patience. They'd both be easier for me if I were a little more crazy—and a little more patient.

Baseball, before the game starts, everybody's playing cards, watching TV, joking around, reading mail, signing balls, maybe even practicing with a bow and arrow. Football, before the game starts, everybody's sitting on the floor, quietly, thinking about whose head they're going to take off. Not me, though. No. I lie on the floor, close my eyes, go to sleep—and dream about whose head I'm going to take off.

During a baseball game, you turn it on—and you turn it off. You concentrate when you're at the plate or on the bases or in the field, but when you come off the field, and it's not your turn to hit, you can go to the locker room, have a burger, talk to your teammates, go to the john, or yell at the other team from the bench. You can relax.

But in football, once the game starts, there's no letup. Even if the other team has the ball, the intensity is there, the adrenaline keeps flowing, you never know when you might have to run back onto the field. You don't get a break until halftime, and then there are coaches cussing and screaming.

Which game do I like better?

I like baseball better in the spring.

I like football better in the fall.

I think I probably relate a little better to football players, but I'm closer to my teammates in baseball. You live in the same hotel with them for eighty or ninety days a year. You see them in the lobby, you see them on the bus, you talk with them during batting practice and during the game. You don't talk much during football practice or during games, and when you go into meetings, you're separated: running backs in one meeting, wide receivers in another, linemen in another. You don't really get to know some of your teammates, especially the defensive players if you're an offensive player. You only spend about ten or twelve days a year living together on the road.

I like most football players and most baseball players, but you get some cowardly lions in both sports. Cowardly lions—that's what I call people who point fingers and blame someone else whenever something goes wrong. They never do anything wrong themselves.

If Bo plays well, that's because of me, and if Bo plays horseshit, that's because of me, too. I don't mean I can do it by myself, I can do it without blockers or anything like that, I just mean that if I don't do my job the way I'm supposed to, it's because I screwed up, not anyone else.

The first game after I joined the Raiders was against Seattle, and the coaches kept me on the bench. They felt it was tough enough getting the veterans going again, after a month on the picket lines, without trying to rush me, too.

The second game, we went to New England to play the Patriots. Marcus Allen started, of course, but I got into the game in the first half. The first time I carried the ball, I ran over a defensive end, ran over a defensive back, almost fumbled, held onto the ball, then dragged a tackler about five yards. I gained fourteen yards on my first run in the NFL. The next time, I ran over a few more people. My third carry, I spun and a guy hit me and split my thumb wide open. I went to the sidelines and said, "Tape it up."

I was scared. I knew I'd have to have stitches at halftime, and I knew they'd have to give me a shot. I'd rather be hit by a defensive tackle. They gave me the shot at halftime and sewed me up, and then in the second half somebody split the thumb open again. I carried the ball a total of eight times, gained thirty-seven yards. It was okay, nothing spectacular.

The next couple of weeks, against Minnesota and San Diego, I started to feel more comfortable in the Raiders' system. I carried the ball more often and averaged more than six yards a carry, still nothing special. When we played in San Diego, I caught up with Lionel James, my former Auburn teammate. The Little Train was a star with the Chargers, a runner, a pass catcher and one of the best punt returners in the league. And he was still only five-foot-six.

The first three games I played were all on the

road, and all defeats. I made my debut at home against the American Conference champions, the Denver Broncos, and for the first time, I was in the starting lineup, playing next to Marcus. In the second quarter, with Denver leading, 13–0, we had the ball on the Broncos' thirty-five-yard line. I got the ball, took a step to my right, pivoted, cut back to the left, got past the line of scrimmage and saw a Denver cornerback, Mike Harden, waiting for me at the thirty-yard line.

"The hell with running around him," I thought, "I'm going right at him."

I didn't want to hurt him. I just wanted to give him a message: "Hey, I'm gonna give you a lick. You ain't gonna hit me. I'm gonna hit you."

He held his ground. It was like stepping in front of a train. I didn't break stride. I ran through him. I raced down to the five-yard line and then dove into the end zone. I had my first NFL touchdown.

The hit on Harden kind of got the attention of all the defensive backs around the league. It got on all the highlight shows, and after that, it seemed like nobody ran right up to me and tried to take my head off. They respected me. They knew I was willing to lower my shoulder and try to put a hole in them.

I ran for another touchdown in the second half, gained 98 yards against Denver in thirteen carries. I didn't feel I was quite as fast as I was at Auburn—I'd lost maybe half a step—but I was a little bigger. I knew I could still play.

Then we went to Seattle. "Monday Night Football." My college roommate, Tommie Agee, was with the Seahawks, but he was sitting out the season with a knee injury. Seattle had Brian Bosworth, a rookie linebacker from Oklahoma who was big and fast and strong and brash. He was getting more attention than any defensive player to come into the league in years.

It was my twenty-fifth birthday, November 30, 1987, and I celebrated. Early in the second quarter, I caught a pass from Marc Wilson for a touchdown. Later in the same quarter, back at our own nine-yard line, I took a pitchout, cut outside and just flat-out sprinted down the sideline. Bosworth had a shot at me. Half a dozen Seahawks had shots at me. None of them came close. I outran all of them. I went 91 yards for a touchdown. I didn't know it was the longest run in the history of the Raiders, the eighth-longest run in the history of the NFL.

In the third quarter, I met Bosworth—head-on. We were on Seattle's two-yard line, and I got the ball and cut to my right, and Boz was waiting for me at the one, planting himself. I wasn't going to get fancy. I went right at him. I went right through him. Just drove him back into the end zone. Boz stood up well after the game. He had no excuses, just a compliment for me. "He ran my butt over," Bosworth said.

I ended up carrying the ball eighteen times and rushing for 221 yards. No one had ever run for more than 200 yards for the Raiders. The roller coaster shot back up again, and people started saying I was better than Jim Brown and O. J. Simpson and Gale Sayers and I should give up baseball and go straight to the Pro Football Hall of Fame, and I just let it all go in one ear and out the other. I don't believe that stuff any more than I believe all the bad things they write about me. I know there's always somebody out there who's better than me. I also know that someday, when I give up one of my two sports, it's going to be football that I give up.

But that game in Seattle was sure fun.

Some people had begun grumbling about my practice habits, my work ethic, but after the Seattle game, Howie Long said to me, "Bo, if I were a coach, you know what I'd tell you?"

"What?" I said.

" 'Fuck practice,' " Howie Long said. " 'Just show up at the stadium on Sunday. That's all I care about.' "

Two weeks later, we went to Kansas City to play the Chiefs. I wasn't worried about the fans. I was kind of looking forward to them. I knew they'd be all over me, but that was okay. I was the enemy now. I wasn't playing for their city.

I also knew that a bunch of my teammates from the Royals would be coming to the game. George Brett was a regular at our games in Los Angeles, and he was flying in from his winter home in Palm Springs. I knew I'd hear at least a few cheers, and if we won, we'd be only one game under .500, and we'd still have an outside chance of making the playoffs.

But when I woke up Sunday morning in our hotel in Kansas City, I had an eerie feeling, like someone was sitting on my shoulder and saying to me, "Something's going to go wrong."

I couldn't shake the feeling.

When we ran onto the field at Arrowhead Stadium, which is right opposite Royals Stadium, separated just by a parking lot, I was greeted by a barrage of baseballs and dozens of signs. Not too many of them were complimentary. A typical one said: RAIDER TRAITOR. Another one showed a jackass named Bo. I liked that one. I think everybody has a little jackass in him.

On our first play from scrimmage, I got the ball and I tried to go around end and I was walled in. Dean Miraldi, one of our guards, a big guy, built like he was made out of marble, was pulling to block, and I was trying to make a move, fake out one of the Chiefs, and Miraldi fell on me, and my right ankle popped, and my first thought was that it was broken.

I got up and went back to the huddle and my foot was numb. I said to myself, "Uh-oh, this isn't happening." I carried the ball a couple of more times, didn't do anything, and then they called a play for me to block. Bill Maas of the Chiefs came up the middle and I tried to plant my foot and hit him, but I couldn't plant it right and he hit me as hard as I've ever been hit. Maas knocked me through the air; it felt like I went twenty yards. At that point, I said, "I can't walk. I'm done." I limped off the field and my day was over.

I told Al Davis afterward that I woke up with a funny feeling that something was going to go wrong, and he said, "If you told me that this morning, I never would have let you play." Sure.

The ankle was sprained—not broken—but since we lost to the Chiefs and didn't have a chance of making the playoffs, the Raiders decided it'd be better if I didn't play the last two games of the season.

So my first NFL season ended in Kansas City. I had played seven games, carried the ball eighty-one times and gained 554 yards, an average of almost 7 yards a carry. Even though I had played less than half a season, I made just about all of the All-Rookie teams, and a couple of football publications named me the NFL's Rookie of the Year.

I went out to dinner with George Brett after the game—I like George so much and I feel sorry for him, too; I wish he'd find a good relationship and settle down—but that wasn't the reason I stayed overnight in Kansas City. I stayed because I was flying to St. Louis the next day. I was going to see a kid in junior college who was having trouble playing basketball because they didn't have shoes big enough for him. I'd heard about him on TV and I'd called Nike and arranged for them to custom-make sneakers for him. I was delivering them myself on Monday—size 19½.

Sunday night, after dinner, I watched television in my hotel room in Kansas City. Mr. Fogelman and John Schuerholz, the general manager of the Royals, and Duke Wathan, who'd taken over as manager late in the 1987 season, were all talking about me. They all said they hoped my ankle wasn't broken. Outside of that, they didn't have too many nice things to say.

Duke said that he figured Gary Thurman was going to be his starting left fielder in 1988. John Schuerholz said he thought that Bo was going to have to spend at least the first half of the 1988 season in Omaha. And Mr. Fogelman said, "Bo is going to have to make a choice. He's got to decide if he's going to play for the Royals or if he's going to be a football player."

I sat in my hotel room, my ankle throbbing, and I listened to all of this.

I haven't spoken to John Schuerholz since. He doesn't even have my home telephone number. (As a matter of fact, neither the Royals nor the Raiders have my home number; if they want to reach me, they have to call Richard Woods.) How do I feel about John Schuerholz? Let's just say that his crackers don't sit well in my bowl of soup.

They had all written me off.

I loved hearing that.

The race was about to begin. Bo Jackson stepped onto the diving board and turned and stared at his opponent. Bo's opponent stared at the water. His tail began to swish. Bo's opponent was an alligator, who was more than nine feet long and weighed close to six hundred and fifty pounds. The gator couldn't wait to dive in.

"Sit!" said Bo, ad-libbing.

Bo and the alligator were filming a commercial, the story line an athletic duel between the two, Bo representing Mountain Dew Sport, a new energy drink, and the gator representing an older, more familiar energy aid.

Bo said he was not worried the first time he saw the gator. "I'm sure he knows who I am," Bo said.

Bo knew who the gator was. He was a movie star, highly acclaimed for his convincing portrayal of an alligator in *Raiders of the Lost Ark*.

Bo is no novice in front of the cameras, either. He is as big on Madison Avenue as he is on the diamond or the gridiron. His commercials for Nike have had the same stunning impact as his ninety-yard touchdown runs and his five hundred-foot home runs.

The marriage between Bo and Nike is one of those rare matches that enhances both parties. The Nike commercials earn both the star and the sneakers a following far beyond the playing field. Women who would not know a Royal from a Raider even if each were in uniform know Bo from his commercials. They are marvels of concept and of execution.

"Bo knows football . . . Bo knows baseball . . . Bo knows basketball" has made "Bo knows" arguably the most pervasive phrase of 1990, surpassing, certainly, any George Bush pronouncement and probably even any Bart Simpson outcry.

And John McEnroe's "Bo knows tennis?" . . . Wayne Gretzky's head-shaking "No" . . . and Bo Diddley's "Bo, you don't know Diddley"—each line delightfully delivered—provide a Bo-deprecating touch that underlines his virtues.

Bo's own lines are lovely, too—"Another day, another hobby" . . . "Air Bo, I like the sound of that" . . . "Now when's that Tour de France thing?"—even though he speaks most eloquently in body language.

The best measure of the power of "Bo knows" may be that it has inspired parodies stretching from the intellectual pages of *The New Yorker* to the comic pages of the daily newspaper. David Racine contributed to *The New Yorker* "Bo Knows Fiction," an account of Bo creating and typing a literary masterwork in a public arena, while Marv Albert offers play-by-play and Joyce Carol Oates color commentary. "I'm thinking we may be looking at some metafiction here," Oates suggests. "Metafiction it is," Albert enthuses. "Nice call, Joyce."

Jeff Millar and Bill Hinds crafted the comic-page

parody in their *Tank McNamara* strip. In one panel, George Bush states, "Bo knows foreign policy," and in the next, Bo asks, "If we win the cold war and lose Gorbachev as leader of socialism, what price victory?" In another panel, Albert Einstein theorizes, "Bo knows particle physics," and in the next, Bo predicts, "The supercolliding superconductor will give us a window onto the creation of the universe."

Somewhere between *The New Yorker* and *Tank,* probably not halfway, *Sports Illustrated* served up a Leigh Montville column in which Bo knowledgeably delivers a baby by cesarean section, shoots the photographs for the magazine's annual swimsuit issue, whittles a bust of Napoleon from a block of wood and cracks up a Las Vegas audience with his stand-up comedy routine.

Bo certainly knows business. He speaks for three of the nation's giant companies, each unmistakably prestigious, in Nike, AT&T and Pepsi-Cola, which markets Mountain Dew Sport, and he also has contracts with Franklin Products, which offers sports equipment such as a Bo Jackson football; Cramer Products, which presents a Bo Jackson line of sports medicine; and Tiger Electronics, which markets a Bo Jackson video game. Add in Club Bo— a fan club with membership applications available on a box of Cheerios—plus countless propositions that Richard Woods keeps weighing and juggling, and you have one of the world's most muscular conglomerates.

Bo does commercials for the same reason he plays baseball and football—"It's fun"—and, of course, he is well compensated for them, even more handsomely than he is for playing baseball and football.

He made his first commercial in 1986, urging young people to say no to cocaine. The commercial was sponsored by Methodist Hospital in Memphis, when Bo was playing for the Chicks. "I was jittery," Bo recalled, as he paused between takes with the gator. "I didn't know what to expect."

"More nervous than the first time you took batting practice with the Royals?"

"I knew I could do batting practice," Bo said. "I didn't know if I could do a commercial."

Now Bo knows he can, and he not only performs without nervousness, he performs without a trace of a speech impediment. "When I'm on camera, I never stutter," Bo said. "I never stutter when I'm angry, either. When I'm angry, I can talk faster than an auctioneer."

Bo's stuttering no longer concerns him. "If it gets worse," he said, "that's fine. If it gets better, that's fine, too. It's not a curse. It's just a speech impediment. I'm not going to worry about it."

Bo does worry about being perfect when he shoots a commercial, mainly because he wants to finish quickly. Since the commercials cut into precious time between games, stealing family time and fishing time, Bo shows up prepared, tries to complete eight-hour shoots in four hours, two-day shoots in one.

He did his part in the Bolympics commercial for Nike without working directly with Kirk Gibson, Jim Everett, Michael Jordan, John McEnroe or Wayne Gretzky—they shot their cameos at *their* convenience—but he did team up with Bo Diddley, the old blues guitarist. They shot their scenes at a nightclub not far from the Royals' spring training headquarters near Orlando. "I liked meeting Bo Diddley," Bo Jackson said. "He *knows* sports."

Bo also enjoyed meeting and working with Sonny Bono, who appeared in Nike's follow-up commercial, the

1990 edition. Why Sonny—and not Cher? *Bo-no. Bo-know.* Get it?

The director of the Nike gems is a perfectionist named Joe Pytka, an enlightened despot who screams at everyone, including Bo. Once Pytka wanted to get a shot of Bo, in football uniform, running right through the camera. He wanted it to look as if Bo were coming through the lens and into the living room. Pytka shot the scene three or four times, and each time, five or six inches from the lens, Bo veered sharply to his left or sharply to his right.

The effect wasn't good enough for Pytka. "C'mon, you sissy," he shouted at Bo. "Run through the damned camera. Run me over. Knock me on my ass."

Bo loves challenges.

The camera was cushioned. It was supposed to protect Pytka. It didn't.

Bo assaulted the camera at full speed, drove the camera back into the director, bowled him over, busted his nose. Pytka got up bloody, looked at Bo, looked at the crew and snapped, "Okay, *that's* a take!"

He had the shot he wanted. He retreated to his trailer, leaving Bo laughing and the crew cheering as if Bo had just scored four touchdowns.

Pytka survived. He is a big man, several inches taller than Bo, who always travels with a basketball. Whenever he gets a break in the shooting, Pytka likes to play basketball. "He can't play worth a damn," Bo said. "He's the one guy in the world I can play better than."

Bo beat the gator, too, in basketball, in the Mountain Dew Sport spot. He also beat the gator in football, baseball and sprinting—Bo's specialties. Their competition was supposed to end with the gator's specialty—swimming.

They stood on adjoining diving boards, poised for the start of their race.

Bo looked at the water, looked again at the alligator, then shook his head.

Un-uh.

See you later.

Bo knows gators.

6 THANK GOD I'M NOT A WOMAN

Was it diving for the touchdown that beat Alabama or hitting the home run off the light tower at Georgia?

Was it running over Mike Harden or over Brian Bosworth?

Was it racing 91 yards for a touchdown or 92?

Was it the throw in Seattle or the home run in the All-Star Game?

People are always asking me what was my biggest thrill, and the answer is easy. I got the biggest thrill of my life on August 2, 1988. I watched my son being born.

Nicholas was born in Kansas City. He wasn't born in Omaha or Memphis or any of the other cities where the Kansas City Royals have farm teams. No matter what the Royals' front-office people were saying all winter, I didn't spend one day of the 1988 season in the minor leagues.

I knew I wasn't going to.

From the day I reported to spring training, I was determined to speak to the Royals with my actions and not with words. I wasn't going to take cheap shots at them in the papers. I wasn't going to sink to their level.

I didn't speak to the media all spring. No interviews. Not one. People knew enough about me already.

I don't especially like to talk to the media anyway. I feed all reporters with a long-handled spoon, and I tell them that every chance I get. I don't consider anybody in the media my friend. You never know when they're going to turn on you for no good reason. That *Sports Illustrated* story when I was in college was the last magazine article about me I ever read. It was garbage. I heard there was a good story in *GQ, Gentlemen's Quarterly*, in 1990. I don't know. I never read it. I know there are good people in the media as well as bad, but I just don't have enough time to sort them out. I don't read the sports pages. I'm not into reading about myself. I'll leave that to people who don't know Bo.

In 1988, in spring training, I went to work early and I stayed late. I spent hour after hour in the batting cage. I hit .333 and led the team in home runs, runs batted in and stolen bases. I just tore up spring training. The Royals waited till the last day to call me in and then John Schuerholz said, "We want you to know we like the way you presented yourself in spring training, we like your work habits, you've done everything we've asked of you, we just wanted to tell you that you've made the team, you're going to Kansas City."

"You assholes," I said, "I knew that from the first day of spring training. You people will never learn."

I didn't say that out loud. I said it to myself.

I like to make people eat their words.

The Royals hadn't even put my picture in their yearbook for 1988.

I had a great season—for fifty games. I stole three bases in one game against Milwaukee. I had four hits in two different games against Boston. In May, I batted .330, with five home runs and nineteen runs batted in. I was named the Royals' Player of the Month.

On May 31, in Cleveland, I hit in my ninth straight game, raised my average to .309, but, beating out a ground ball to the shortstop, ripped my left hamstring muscle. I crossed first base and went down. I was able to get up and walk back to the dugout without much pain, so at first I thought it was just a minor pull.

But that night my leg swelled up so much it looked like a balloon and it felt like a sandbag. I couldn't lift it, and no matter how many pain pills I took, it still hurt. I went on the disabled list and missed the whole month of June. They brought Gary Thurman up from Omaha to take my place.

I couldn't have picked a worse time to get hurt. I was still striking out a lot, but I was beginning to put things together. I had nine home runs, thirty runs batted in, fourteen stolen bases, all in less than a third of the season.

The pitchers were working harder on me. They were brushing me back off the plate. I accept that. That's part of the game. Move me back. But don't throw at my head. That's a cardinal sin. Don't even think of it, because if you try to hurt me, I'm going to hurt you. If you start something with me, you better pack a lunch. You could be in for a fight that'll make World War II look like a game of jacks.

The pitcher is the enemy. He's like the defensive back or the linebacker in football. He's not trying to hurt you, like they are, but he's trying to fool you, to embarrass you. He wants you to expect the wrong pitch or chase a bad pitch. It's a mind game.

I like facing Dave Stewart, Nolan Ryan, Roger Clemens, not because they're easy to hit—they're not—but because they come right at you. They're not going to pussyfoot around with pitches in the dirt. They're not going to throw doo-doo. They come right at you with the fastball, with their best pitch, and they say, "Hit it if you can. If you miss it, you miss it, and if you jump on it, let's see how far it goes." Those are the guys I like to face, not the ones who can throw a ninety-mile-an-hour fastball, but instead throw doo-doo at you, change-ups and slow curves, and then try to sneak the fastball past you.

I like guys to challenge me, to go with their strength. When I face Charlie Hough, I go up there looking for a knuckleball. The last thing I'm looking for is a fastball. It would piss me off if Charlie Hough threw me ten straight fastballs. I want to see his best stuff.

On July 2, I got back in the lineup, but I never got back in the groove I had in May. I had a few good moments, that was all. In the middle of July, in Boston, I made the best catch I'd made in the big leagues, throwing myself through the air to grab a line drive hit by Rich Gedman, and I hit one of my longest home runs, high off the center-field wall in Fenway Park.

A couple of weeks later, in Baltimore, I was batting against the Orioles' Jeff Ballard, and I stepped out of the box and called timeout. But as I did, I saw that Ballard was already into his windup, so I jumped back in, didn't even get set, swung and hit the ball over the right-center-field fence.

I didn't run. I turned around and looked at the umpire. I didn't know whether he had called timeout or not. He gave me a "Don't look at me" look, so I ran out the home run. My teammates were rolling in the dugout. We started a four-game winning streak that night.

The streak ended August 2 against Detroit. I missed the start of the game because I was at the hospital, holding my new son.

I took Linda to the hospital at nine-thirty in the morning. They took blood from her, gave her a bunch of tests and then, around noontime, gave her a shot to induce labor. She started having contractions around one o'clock, and for five hours, I held her hand and kissed her cheek and listened to her moans and told her that everything was going to be all right. I even went and lied to her. "Baby," I said, "I'm never going to put you through this again."

A few minutes after six, Nicholas started to come out. It was the most remarkable thing I ever saw in my life. I'd never experienced anything like it. It was so touching and humbling and wonderful, and I started to cry. Through it all, I kept thinking, "Thank God I'm not a woman. I don't think I could handle that."

Nicholas was so ugly when he came out, he looked like he was dipped in glue. Then the nurse cleaned him off, and he looked beautiful, and I thought about the miracle I had performed. I had produced two children—that was the miracle. Of course, Linda had something to do with it, too.

The nurse handed Nicholas to me, and I didn't

want to give him back. I wanted to hold him forever. I wanted to wrap my arms around him and keep him warm and safe. Linda told me afterward she saw the look on my face and the way I was holding the baby and she fell in love with me all over again.

Finally the nurse took Nicholas from me and put him in the nursery, and they took Linda back to her room, and I went to the ballpark. I got there in time to pinch-hit. It was the bottom of the ninth inning, and we were losing, 1–0.

Someday I may tell Nicholas that I hit a home run in the bottom of the ninth inning to tie up the game to celebrate his birth.

I may tell him some other lies, too.

Actually, I got hit by a pitch. But the umpire called it strike two. The next pitch was a bad one, too, and the umpire called it strike three.

I didn't even argue. I went inside, got dressed and rushed back to the hospital. Linda was awake. She told me she was hungry, she hadn't eaten any dinner. So I went out and found a place that was open and brought back two cheeseburgers and two orders of fries and climbed in bed next to Linda and ate dinner with her.

A nurse spotted me. "What are you doing in there?" she said.

"Not what you're thinking," I said.

For the second year in a row, a lot of people said I had a terrible second half of the season. I don't think so. I married Linda in the second half of the 1987 season, and Nicholas was born in the second half of

I always tried to be inconspicuous on the Auburn campus.

Courtesy Rich Addicks/*Atlanta Journal*

I don't mind signing autographs in the right place at the right time—for the right person.

Courtesy Kansas City Royals

I took a good look at my first home run in the big leagues; they said it was the longest in the history of Royals Stadium.

Courtesy Kansas City Royals

I hope George Steinbrenner was watching when I made this catch against the New York Yankees. If I was ever traded to Steinbrenner's team, I'd quit baseball.

© 1988 AP/Worldwide Photo

When I strike out, I feel like throwing a bat or a helmet or the water cooler.

UPI/Bettmann Newsphotos

I don't know much about history, but I know these players from the old Negro Leagues opened doors for those of us who came later.

Courtesy Kansas City Royals

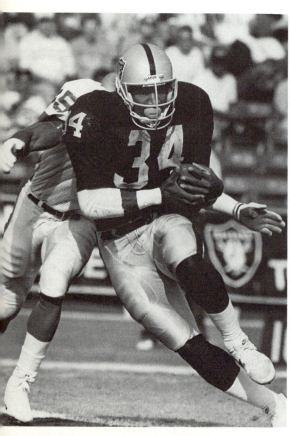

If my mother put
on a helmet and
shoulder pads and a
uniform that wasn't
the same as the one
I was wearing, I'd
run over her if she
was in my way. And
I love my mother.

Courtesy Los Angeles Raiders

It looks like Billy Crystal just hit one to East Hell. Photo by Bill Sumner

Joe Pytka, who directs the Nike commercials, is the one guy in the world I can beat at basketball.

Photo by Bob Peterson

Let me tell you: Bo Diddley knows sports. Photo by Bill Sumner

I know that I don't know as much as some people think I know.

Tank McNamara Copyright © 1990 Universal Press Syndicate. Reprinted with permission. All rights reserved.

We did it: Linda, Spud, Nick and I judged the JUST DO IT poster contest.

Courtesy Nareshimah Osei

BO KNOWS FOOTBALL

BO KNOWS BASKETBALL. TOO

BO KNOWS TENNIS?

"NO"

BO KNOWS CRICKET

BO KNOWS SOCCER

BO KNOWS BASEBALL

"BO. YOU DON'T KNOW DIDDLEY"

My next hobby is going to be bobsledding, but I'm not sure whether I'm going to win the gold medal in the Olympics in 1992 or in 1994.

Photo of Football Bo by Bill Sumner. All other photos by Bob Peterson.

the 1988 season. I wish I had done half as well on the baseball field.

Still, even though my average slipped to .246, I was the first player in the history of the Kansas City Royals to hit twenty-five home runs and steal twenty-five bases in the same season. And I led all the Royals' outfielders by throwing out eleven base runners. On the minus side, I tied a Kansas City record by striking out nine straight times in the middle of September, but that was nothing compared to my twenty-one straight strikeouts when I was a freshman at Auburn.

When the baseball season ended, I took my ten days off and didn't even think about football, didn't look at a playbook, didn't talk to the Los Angeles coaches. I just relaxed with my family. Then I reported to the Raiders, got my stuff, threw it in my locker, went to my first meeting, went to sleep, woke up, got my stuff and went out and began banging heads.

After just three days of meetings and practices, I flew back to Kansas City—to play against the Chiefs. The fans weren't as hard on me this time. They booed, of course, but they didn't throw baseballs. The Chiefs weren't as tough on me, either. I got through the game without injury. I played the whole game, carried the ball twenty-one times, caught two passes, gained 70 yards rushing and scored the last touchdown in a 27–17 victory. I was a football player again.

The next week, against New Orleans, I carried the ball the first two plays of the game, ran for 20 yards and 25—and pulled a hamstring. I didn't try to be a hero. I sat out the rest of the game and was ready to play the following week—against the Chiefs again, this time in Los Angeles.

We beat them again. I scored the first touchdown

of the game on a 22-yard run, which turned out to be the longest touchdown run of the season for me and for the Raiders. I rushed seventeen times, gained 80 yards and caught one pass. We won, 17–10.

I love to play against the Chiefs. It's fun, knowing that I'm playing for the city—and against it. I see a lot of the Chiefs around the Kansas City Sports Complex during the last couple of months of the baseball season, and they're nice guys. But not on the field. On the field, you have no friends except the guys who are blocking for you. The other guys are mortal enemies. The same ones who give me a big smile outside Royals Stadium in September will try to tear my head off in October.

The victory over the Chiefs was the start of a three-game winning streak which was capped by a 9–3 victory over San Francisco, the team that went on to win the Super Bowl. We beat the 49ers on their field, and all my teammates were talking about afterward was that I ran over Ronnie Lott. I ran over his ass twice. It was no big deal. "Look," I said, "if my mother put on a helmet and shoulder pads and a uniform that wasn't the same as the one I was wearing, I'd run over *her* if she was in my way." And I don't love Ronnie Lott.

After the San Francisco game, we had a winning record—for the first time since I'd joined the Raiders—and a good shot at the playoffs. The Raiders hadn't been in the playoffs since 1985, and you could see how badly Al Davis wanted it. He was very proud of the fact that the Raiders had the best won-lost record of any big league team—baseball, basketball, football or hockey—over the past quarter of a century. He didn't like losing.

I like Al Davis. He accepts me for what I am. He doesn't feel he has to change me. He believes that I can help his team playing two thirds of a season, and that's what he asks of me. I think Al Davis is a nice man, even though every other word out of his mouth is a swearword. You can't change him. You can't even change the way he dresses. He always wears bell-bottom white pants, black patent-leather shoes and either a white jacket or a black jacket. He wears clean white pants every single day. All of his players wonder how many pairs of white pants he has.

We didn't make the playoffs in 1988. We fell apart, lost four of our last five games, two of them to the Seattle Seahawks. If we had won those two, we would've finished first in our division. In the two games put together, I gained only 98 yards, less than half of what I'd gained in one game against the Seahawks in 1987.

I ended up with an unspectacular season—580 yards rushing on 136 carries, an average of only 4.3 yards a carry, the lowest of my life, professional, college or high school. I didn't break a big run all year. Still, I had no regrets about playing two sports. It was fun. It would've been more fun if the Royals and the Raiders were winning, but it was still fun.

After the football season ended, I did get a couple of months off. I didn't pick up a baseball or a bat or a glove or a weight. The only time I even put on sneakers was when I went fishing. The rest of the time I wore my hunting boots.

Playing football and baseball does cut into the time I can spend hunting and fishing, but I'm not complaining. I still get to use my rods and my bows and my arrows sometimes, and this way I don't have any desire to go partying or to hang out, not during the playing seasons, and not afterward.

Playing two sports professionally keeps me out of trouble.

19 years old and going nowhere,
I got a ride to Bessemer and walked
the night road toward Birmingham
passing dark groups of men cursing
the end of a week like every week . . .
South, the lights of Bessemer glowed
as though a new sun rose there . . .
                    A life
was calling to be lived, but how
and why I still had to learn

                    —Philip Levine
                    from "At Bessemer"

As usual, the news spread quickly: Bo was home. Bo Jackson was back in Bessemer. Alfred Mack, younger brother of Keith Mack, who ran in the McAdory High backfield with Bo, was one of the first to spot him. "H-h-hey, B-B-Boo," Alfred Mack called. "Wha-wha-whatcha d-d-doin' h-h-home?"

When they were children, Alfred Mack used to mock Bo's speech impediment. Alfred was able to get away with it, without being smashed by a fist or a rock, because his brother was Bo's best friend. But Bo always warned Alfred, "One day you're gonna stutter."

Now Alfred Mack stutters. "Worse than I did as a kid," Bo Jackson says. "And nobody else in his family stutters."

Bo waved to Alfred. "Wha-wha-whatcha d-d-doin', m-m-man?" Bo said.

"C-c-come o-o-over h-h-here," Alfred Mack shouted back, "an-an-and I-I-I'll k-k-kick your ass!"

Bo Jackson laughed, walked over to Alfred Mack and slapped hands. Alfred, one year younger than Bo, showed Bo pictures of his five children.

Bo was, as always, glad to be visiting Bessemer, back among friends and family. "I always say I'm gonna rest when I come here," Bo said, "and I never do. I try to see as many of my old friends as I can."

The city has changed since Bo left. It is even more depressed economically. The mills are shut down. The drive-in theater, where Bo sat on the hood of his sister's Buick and ate popcorn and watched his first movie, *Death Race 2000,* switched to Triple-X-rated films before it turned into a shopping mall. The Raimond Elementary School is abandoned, but when Bo jogs past it, during his gentle off-season workouts, he remembers the time the blue Mustang stopped, and the high school kids spilled out to chase him and call him names. The courthouse, the tallest building in Bessemer, no longer looms so large.

Bo still has relatives and friends in Bessemer who have never been out of Alabama, who have never flown in an airplane, whose worlds still stop at the horizon. "People here don't know about rental cars," Bo said. "When I come here, I fly into Atlanta and I rent a Lincoln or a Cadillac, something big enough for the whole family, and people here think I own all those cars. 'Man, where you getting all these *bad* cars?' they ask me. They also ask me about the women in California, and I tell them, 'There are beautiful women everywhere. But it's too crowded out there, you wouldn't like it.' I don't want to make them—or me—feel bad because I'm not in Bessemer any more."

In Bessemer, Bo visited his past.

He visited his father, Big Track Adams, and his father's wife and their children. Bo has a half-brother who could be his twin. The same face exactly. "I love my father," Bo said, "and I think I even understand him now."

He visited the mother and grandmother of his high

school girlfriend and showed them photographs of Garrett and Nicholas. "Marilyn is one of the few girls I ever dated who is still my friend," Bo said. "Maybe the only one. She's married now, but she's my friend. All the other girls I dated are now my mortal enemies. We don't come within ten miles of each other."

Whose fault?

"Mine," Bo said. "For seeing them too long."

He visited the home of Steve Mann, the ambidextrous quarterback who beat him out for the student-athlete award when they were seniors at McAdory High. Bo knocked on the door, then pushed it open and let out the Auburn battle cry—"Warrrr Eagle!" The Manns knew who had come calling. "Steve's dad is a diehard 'Roll, Tide!' fan," Bo explained.

He visited his former high school coach, Dick Atchison, another Alabama fan. "I love him anyway," Bo said.

He visited Victor Williams, Ricky Johnson, T. C. Scott, a small army of old friends, The Bicycle Bandits and The Pig Killers. "Hey, Bo," one of them said. "When you were growing up, we could hardly get you to say two words. Now you're on TV, fooling all those people, taking their money."

"Yeah, Bo," another friend said. "You a movie star now. But remember when you hit Bobby in the head with a rock because he wouldn't give you a quarter?"

Bo nodded. He remembered.

He visited his oldest brother, Anthony, and his youngest brother, Clarence, and his older brother Jerry, who once helped fix up their sister's Buick Riviera. The three brothers were living in Bessemer; so were four of Bo's sisters. "I hug my sisters when I see them," Bo said. "But my brothers, we don't hug; we don't feel right hugging. But we are glad to see each other."

And, of course, he visited his mother. She is the real reason he returns to Bessemer, the reason he brings his wife and his children to the city he escaped. When he was a child, his mother was sagely stern with him, but she has no cherry switch, no extension cord for Garrett and Nicholas. "She spoils them rotten," Bo said. "She gets them strung out on junk food. She gives them everything they want. My kids think it's paradise."

Bo, in turn, spoils his nieces and nephews, the twenty-eight children of his brothers and sisters. He herds them to the shopping mall and wipes out the local stock of Nintendo cartridges. But if Bo is the generous uncle, he is also demanding. He does not want his nieces and nephews to be, as he once was, the bad Jackson kid.

As always, Bo checked out the collection of guns, perhaps twenty of them, that he keeps at his mother's home. He noticed one gun was missing, a nickel-plated .38 with a rubber grip. "Like the state troopers use," Bo said.

Bo suspected one of his older nephews. He called one of his sisters and asked her to look through the boy's room. She found the pistol and a handful of bullets.

Bo drove to her house, picked up the gun and the bullets and went to the high school. He stopped along the way to call the principal and ask him to bring his nephew to Coach Atchison's office.

The youngster came in.

"Have you seen my pistol?" Bo asked.

"What pistol?" the kid asked.

"My .38," Bo said. "The one that's been hanging on Mom's bedpost for four years."

"No, I ain't seen it."

"Don't lie to me," Bo said. "Please don't lie to me."

"I told you I ain't seen your pistol."

Bo pulled the bullets out of his pocket, slammed them on the coach's desk and smacked his nephew across the face.

"That's enough, Bo," the principal said, and Bo stepped back.

"Mom don't need to be worrying about things like that," Bo said later. "There have been four drive-by shootings in Bessemer the last few weeks. For no good reason. Four shootings.

"Trouble today is a whole lot worse than it was fifteen years ago. We threw rocks, we had fights, we killed pigs. But we didn't have crack, we didn't carry knives or guns, we didn't steal cars. That's what they do now. It's scary. I don't want any part of that."

Soon after, Bo left Bessemer—again.

7

GARRETT JACKSON, MEET MICHAEL JACKSON

I went into a slump in 1989. For the first time in four years, I went through a whole year without getting married or having a child. But there were a few consolations: I had my best season in baseball, I had my best season in football, I turned down an invitation to play in the International Basketball Association, I accepted an invitation to take my first ride in a fighter jet and I won the Buckmasters championship.

The Buckmasters is a deer-hunting competition that is held in Alabama in January. You're allowed two shots, and you've got five days to take them, and you can use either a rifle and two bullets or a bow and two arrows. I used a rifle, and I shot the largest deer, a twelve-point buck. I won a trophy and a fifty-dollar side bet from my roommate at the Buckmasters, Wade Boggs.

Then I raced against one of the other hunters, Davey Allison, the stock-car champion. We drove four-wheel motorbikes through an obstacle course, and when I beat Allison, I knew I was in for a good year.

A few weeks later, I took a faster ride. The Kansas Air Guard took me up in an F-16. I had done a PSA—a public service announcement—for them during the 1988 baseball season, and when they offered to pay me, I said "Keep your money. Just take me up in one of your jets."

They did, and I loved it. We did dives. We did loops. It's hard to put it in words, but I got a bigger rush out of flying in an F-16 than I could ever get out of drugs. You don't show it on your face, but the whole time you're up, you're smiling on the inside.

The F-16 is sort of the sports car of military jets. It has all the power of the F-4, but it's smaller and it makes tighter turns. The F-16 pilots like to say that the F-4s are the Cadillacs of the fighter jets, built for comfort, not combat, and the F-4 pilots come back and say that the F-16s are just toys. I'm an F-16 man.

At the end of February, I went to spring training, and the first week we played the Boston Red Sox at our park, Baseball City Stadium, and Oil Can Boyd pitched for the Sox. He and I had a talk before the game, and he said, "Bo, you and I are both from the South, you from 'Bama and me from Mississippi, and we're just country boys who like to eat Southern food, right?"

I said, "Right," and he said, "I am The Can, and I am going to come right at you with my best shit, and if you hit it, I want to see how far Bo Jackson can hit the Oil Can.''

He saw. I hit his first pitch over the 71-foot-high scoreboard in straightaway center field. The ball landed 515 feet from home plate.

The first week of the regular season, we played the Red Sox again, in Kansas City. Roger Clemens started against us and struck me out my first time up, the eighth time he'd struck me out in twelve at-bats against him. My second time up, I fouled off a few curveballs, fouled off a couple of fastballs and then struck out again. Nine for thirteen. "I'll get him next time," I said when I got back to the bench.

The next time, Clemens threw me a ninety-three-mile-an-hour fastball, up high, on the outside part of the plate, and I was waiting for it and I hit a line drive over the right-center-field fence, my first home run of the season. "He hit the ball so hard I couldn't even turn around to see it go over the fence," Clemens said.

One week in April, I hit three home runs, stole five bases, scored six runs, drove in seven and was named the American League's Player of the Week. It was the first time I'd ever been Player of the Week.

On May 9, against Cleveland in Kansas City, in the bottom of the seventh inning, I struck out with two men on base. I was so angry, so frustrated, I turned and, without even thinking about it, snapped my bat over my thigh. The bat split right in half. Afterward, reporters asked me if it was the first time I'd ever broken a bat over my thigh.

"I broke an aluminum bat over my knee in college," I said.

I was just kidding.

The following week, I did something else that I'd never done before. During batting practice, in Minneapolis, I jumped into the cage and, batting left-handed, just for fun, hit a ball 450 feet into the upper deck in right-center field. They told me it was 30 feet short of the longest home run ever hit in the Metrodome.

Kirby Puckett of the Twins was watching. He broke up laughing. "Give me a break," he said.

The next night, batting right-handed, I hit a home run more than 400 feet into the upper deck in right field, which no right-handed batter had ever done before. I didn't really hit it that well. I hit it off the end of the bat. But I did steal home the same night.

I was on a roll. A week later, I was in Texas, facing Nolan Ryan. I was batting cleanup for the first time in the big leagues. The last time we played the Rangers, which was the first time I faced Ryan, he struck me out four times in a row, blew the ball past me. He made it five in a row, then six. Then I came up for a third time. It was the fifth inning, two out, runners on first and third.

Ryan threw the first pitch high and tight, and I fouled it off, and he looked at me like, "You're not supposed to touch that ball. How in hell did you get your bat on that?" The second pitch was higher and tighter, and I just ducked and the ball went over my head. Some reporters thought he was trying to hit me. But I didn't think so. If Ryan wanted to hit me, he would've. He was just trying to get me off the plate. I stepped back in.

The count went to three-and-two. I took my bat, hit the plate with it, then hit my helmet and said to myself, "All right, come on." The next pitch he threw a ninety-one-mile-an-hour fastball, and I swung and— *pow!* The stands got quiet, and the ball sailed over the left-center-field fence. They said it was the longest home run in the history of Arlington Stadium. They said it traveled 461 feet, but I know that as hard as Nolan threw it, and as hard as I swung, it went farther. Before I even got out of the batter's box, the ball was beating the seats way up in left-center field. I got all of it.

It's fun hitting home runs, especially the long ones, but to me it's a lot more fun making a good throw. I just like to show runners that they can't take an extra base on me. I guess the throw I made on June 5 in Seattle, bottom of the tenth inning, score tied, was the best one I've made. Scott Bradley lined the ball into the left-field corner, and I just took the carom off the wall, turned and threw. Bob Boone caught the throw on the fly and tagged out Harold Reynolds at the plate, and we went on to win the game in thirteen innings. Everybody made a big deal about the throw. Duke Wathan said it was the best he'd ever seen, and Reynolds said it was superhuman, and Brett and Boone kept talking about it for days. The thing I liked was that it was a challenge—to make the perfect throw to save the game.

Everybody got excited a few days later when, after grounding out to the pitcher in Milwaukee, I broke my bat in half once again, this time over my head. On my helmet, actually.

The word got around that the bat was already cracked, which it was, but it was only a hairline fracture and that wasn't where I split the bat. The bat had a thin handle and I put it on my helmet and got my neck stiff and pulled down with both hands, and the bat just gave way.

When we came back to Kansas City, there was a reunion at Royals Stadium of players from the old Negro Leagues. I went out to take pictures of the old-timers with my video camera. I was wearing my baseball cap backward, clowning around, and one of them said to me, "Hey, are you Bo Jackson?"

I said I was, and he said, "I'm Ernie Banks," and then he introduced me to the guy who was standing with him, who was Hank Aaron, both of them Hall of Famers. Aaron, who's from Mobile, said to me, "Where you from?"

"Bessemer," I said.

And Aaron called over another old player, a man named Piper Davis, who was from Bessemer, too.

I enjoyed meeting the old players. I wanted to talk to them, shake their hands, show them that I respected them. I don't know much about history, of baseball or anything else, black or white, but I do know these men opened doors, made it easier for those of us who came later.

I'd heard that in some cities the young black players didn't make the old-timers feel very welcome, didn't even bother to talk to them. I asked all of them to autograph a bat for me, and then I gave each of them one of my autographed bats. I was just showing them the kind of respect I'd like to be shown.

The season was going perfectly until, on June 24, I tore something in my quadriceps, the muscle in front of my left thigh. We were playing the Yankees in the rain in Kansas City. Don Mattingly came to bat, and I played him shallow because I knew, with the wind blowing in, he couldn't hit the ball over my head. Don blooped one down the left-field line and I went after it and, as I stretched for it, the quads popped. I actually heard the *pop!*—and felt it. I slowed down and the ball fell fair and rolled to the fence. I went and got it and threw it to Kevin Seitzer and he relayed the ball and got Mattingly at the plate, trying for an inside-the-park home run.

I left the game, and I probably should've gone on the disabled list right away and let it heal. The tear had to hurt my running. But I was hitting good, and we were only one game out of first place, so I said, "The hell with it," and kept on playing.

Ten days later, on the Fourth of July, in our eighty-first game, exactly halfway through the season, I hit two home runs against Oakland. That gave me twenty for the year. I also had twenty stolen bases, and sportswriters were talking about a forty–forty season, which no one had ever done till Jose Canseco did it in 1988. I couldn't get excited about it myself. I'm just not that big on statistics. I can tell when I'm playing well, and when I'm not, without looking at the numbers.

I still don't know how many votes I got for the All-Star Game, but I know it was more than any other player in the American League.

It was fun going to Anaheim for the All-Star Game. I took Linda with me, and except for the women who kept calling my room—Linda was ready to kick ass—we had a good time. I did the Arsenio Hall show, and before the taping, he came backstage and talked with Linda and me. He's a nice guy, really down to earth. You'd never know he's as famous as he is just by sitting down and talking with him.

I enjoy being around good athletes, and we had plenty of them on the American League team, so many that Tony La Russa, who's probably the most respected manager in baseball today, decided to have me lead off. He said he wanted to stir up some excitement.

I was pumped, partly because it was my first All-Star Game and mostly because, right before the game, four F-4 fighter jets in tight formation flew by the stadium. They weren't F-16s, but they still got me going.

The National League scored two runs off Dave Stewart in the top of the first inning and had two men in scoring position, with two out, when Pedro Guerrero hit a line drive into left-center field. I made the catch on the run and trotted off the field, my quads throbbing.

Rick Reuschel was the starting pitcher for the National League, and they told me he throws mostly doo-doo. I went up, looking for a slow pitch. I told myself, "The first slow pitch I get, I'm going to swing out of my ass."

All I wanted was some doo-doo close to the plate, and when I got it, on Reuschel's second pitch, I just golf-swung, like I was hitting the ball off a tee. It was a lucky swing. I didn't get all of it. But I got enough. I hit the ball 448 feet to dead-center field. I was the fifth player ever to lead off for his team with a home run in the All-Star Game. Somebody told me that the other four—Frankie Frisch, Lou Boudreau, Willie Mays and Joe Morgan—were all in the Hall of Fame.

"Goddamn, Bojack, what did you do to that ball?" Kirby Puckett wanted to know after I'd circled the bases.

"Oh, Bo Diddley," said Devon White of the Angels.

"You got the MVP thing wrapped up," someone else yelled.

Then Wade Boggs, batting second, also hit a home run, and the guys started yelling at him that he had the MVP wrapped up.

In the second inning, I came up again, with runners on first and third, one out, the score still tied, 2–2. I hit a ground ball to Ozzie Smith at short, and he flipped to Ryne Sandberg for the force at second, and even though my quadriceps were starting to kill me, I outran the relay to first base, preventing the double play.

I got credit for a run batted in, and that put us ahead for good. Then, my thigh aching, I stole second base. I was in agony, but, hey, it was the All-Star Game. I didn't tell anyone I was in pain.

I got another hit, a single, and when La Russa took me out of the game after six innings, I went right to the clubhouse and put an ice pack on my leg. I was still sitting with the ice pack when Dean Vogelaar, the director of public relations for the Royals, came and told me that I'd been elected MVP. I couldn't even bend over to put my cleats back on, so I just went out to get the award with my shower shoes on.

I found out I was only the second player to hit a home run *and* steal a base in an All-Star Game. The first was Willie Mays, who grew up only ten or fifteen miles from me, in Birmingham.

During the game, in the fourth inning, the people who were watching us on television got to see the Nike Bolympics commercial for the first time, the one with Bo Diddley and Gretzky and Jordan and McEnroe and Gibson and the other athletes. The reaction was about the same as it was to my home run. Everyone went crazy.

Just a few weeks earlier, the Nike commercial in which I rode a bicycle and asked, "When is that Tour de France thing?" won a Clio Award, which is like an Oscar for advertising. The Bo Diddley spot was even better, I thought. I must've watched it fifty times.

The Nike people couldn't have been happier. The sales of their fitness shoes, the cross-training shoes, were soaring, and the combination of the All-Star commercial and my All-Star performance figured to drive the sales up even more. "Cross-training is the rocket here at Nike," said Liz Dolan, their director of public relations, "and Bo's on it."

"As soon as I saw him hit that first-inning home run," said Scott Bedbury, Nike's advertising director, "I knew this was going to be an amazing night. It's like the moon and the stars had to be in some kind of special alignment."

We got a four-star review in *Advertising Age*, which is sort of like *The Sporting News* of advertising. The reviewer called the commercial "this unequivocally magnificent piece of advertising . . . thanks in no small part to the bona fide versatility of Bo Jackson . . . a mercurial egomaniac . . ."

I liked most of it.

Everything was good—except the quadriceps. I started hurting again the first game after the All-Star break, at Yankee Stadium, and then, a week later, against Cleveland, I aggravated the injury and had to be replaced by a pinch-runner. Bret Saberhagen ran for me. I saw him coming out of the dugout with his helmet on, and I thought, "The world's got to be coming to an end if a pitcher's running for me." And of all people, it had to be Saberhagen. I knew then I'd never hear the end of it.

I finally told them to put me on the disabled list a few days later. I wasn't doing myself or the Royals any good. I missed the last week of July and the first week of August, and by the time I came back, my chances for a forty-forty season were gone. I was still afraid to run flat-out.

In mid-August, in Toronto, I broke one more bat over my knee. With the bases loaded, one out and the score tied, I struck out on a pitch that was nowhere near the strike zone. As I turned to splinter the bat, the ball got away from the catcher, and the tie-breaking run came in.

We won that game, the start of a stretch in which we won sixteen out of nineteen and, by September 1, moved to within a game and a half of first place. Saberhagen was pitching unbelievably; he won eight games in a row. On the field, he is one hell of a pitcher. Off the field, sometimes I would like to choke him. He has a sign in his locker that says: I DON'T GIVE A SHIT WHAT YOU SAY, I REFUSE TO GROW UP. He should.

Tom Gordon was pitching great, too. Flash won five out of six decisions in August. He was still only twenty-one years old and looked younger. He is kind of like Nolan Ryan trapped in a five-foot-seven frame. He says he's five-foot-nine, but he's lying. Still, he can throw a fastball in the nineties. He says he's the toughest man in baseball, pound for pound, and at a hundred and sixty pounds, he probably is.

When he first joined us, he lived with me and Linda and the kids. We gave him the guest room, and I treated him like a son. He grew up in Florida, didn't have much of anything and has a tendency to spend all of his money. So I took his paychecks away from him, put them in the bank for him and issued him a little allowance every now and then. I'm kidding. Flash is a bachelor, and I don't recommend him getting married within the next twenty years, because it may take him that long to sow all his wild oats. He keeps begging me to introduce him to people in Hollywood. He says he's ready to do movies and commercials.

We never did catch the Oakland A's. We finished second, seven games behind them. I had personal highs for batting average, home runs, runs batted in, runs scored, hits and strikeouts. I guess the best number was the runs batted in, 105, fourth in the league. I had my second straight season of more than twenty-five home runs and more than twenty-five stolen bases, and I made *USA Today*'s American League All-Star team. I felt I was improving.

Ten days after the baseball season ended, I reported to the Raiders' headquarters in El Segundo. The Raiders had a new coach, Art Shell, which was something they needed badly. They also needed a running back badly. Marcus Allen had banged up his knee two days earlier, in a Monday night game against the New York Jets, and he was out for at least six weeks, maybe for the rest of the season.

Shell didn't have much choice. He put me right to work. After three days of practice, I played most of the next game. For the second year in a row, my first game back was against Kansas City, in Los Angeles, and after a slow start, I wound up gaining 85 yards in eleven carries. We beat the Chiefs.

The next week, the earthquake hit the Bay Area and shook Candlestick Park, and my first reaction was "Thank God I'm not there." Then I started worrying about my friends who were there, Mark McGwire with the A's and Steve Wallace, from Auburn, with the 49ers and some friends who lived right near the Marina, the section of San Francisco that suffered the worst damage.

Games didn't seem so important that week, but we still had to play. I hated leaving my family in our rented home in California while we went to Philadelphia. The Eagles' coach, Buddy Ryan, made a crack before the game that if he were my father, as good as I can hit a baseball, he wouldn't let me play against the Philadelphia defense. It was nice of him to be so concerned, but I don't know what he was worrying about. They didn't hit nearly as hard as I expected them to. Still, they beat us by three points.

The World Series resumed the next week, and while the A's finished off the Giants in San Francisco, we played at home, against the Washington Redskins. I gained a lot of yards and I lost a lot of respect for Dexter Manley, their defensive end. I'd always looked up to Dexter. I liked watching him play. I admired his aggressiveness. This was the first time I played against him, and the first time we ran the ball, I blocked him and knocked him on his ass. Another time, I ran right over him. We were just going up and down the field, and he wasn't tackling anybody.

But that wasn't what lowered my opinion of Dexter. Anybody can have a bad day. But on one play, when I was tackled, he jumped onto the pile and started mouthing off. "Somebody bone his ass," Dexter said. "Bone him in the mouth. Bone him in the eye." He meant that somebody ought to jam an elbow—a bone—into my mouth or my eye.

"Look, man," I said, "you shouldn't wish bad things on people because bad things can happen to you."

Two weeks later, Dexter Manley was out of the NFL; he failed the drug test. As angry as I was at him, I hope he makes it back. I hope he puts his life together.

The Sacramento Kings of the National Basketball Association had an auction to raise money for the Red Cross Northern California Earthquake Relief Fund, and I autographed one of my Raider jerseys—and contributed it. There were some pretty good items in the auction—an autographed baseball from Willie Mays, an autographed photograph from Magic Johnson, an autographed football from Joe Montana, an autographed basketball from Michael Jordan—but I beat them all. My jersey drew top dollar. Somebody paid $3,600 for it.

I went through my first earthquake during the 1989 season—my first, Linda's second. She experienced one when I was on the road. Three o'clock one morning, I felt a tremor and woke up, and the bed started sliding across the room, and I jumped up and said, "Linda? Linda? Do you hear that? That's an earthquake."

And she said, "Uh-huh," and turned over and went back to sleep. I got up, I put on my gym shorts and I went to check on Nick and Spud. They were fast asleep, snoring. I stayed up the rest of the night, waiting for the next tremor, and Linda and the kids slept right through.

As much as I love the West Coast, I'll never move there, just because of the earthquakes. I couldn't live there year-round. I'm nervous enough being out there from October till the end of December. You can't outrun an earthquake.

I went on Arsenio's show again, and this time I brought Spud with me. I got a few cheers when I told Arsenio, "The critics out there who think Bo should do this, and Bo should do that, to make a long story short, they can go to hell!" But Spud stole the show. He told Arsenio that Paula Abdul was his girlfriend and he danced around the stage. A couple of days later, we got a phone call telling us that Michael Jackson had seen Spud with Arsenio and wanted to meet him. Michael Jackson wanted to meet Garrett Jackson.

We were invited to a recording studio in Burbank, where Michael Jackson was working on a new album, and I think I was more impressed by meeting him than Spud was. I was surprised that Michael was so tall, about the same height that I am, and that he had big hands, bigger than mine. He seemed like a nice guy, but I was kind of awed. Spud just said, "Hi, Michael," as though he meets a Michael Jackson every day of the week.

As a matter of fact, during a two-week period, Spud met Michael Jackson, Magic Johnson, Arsenio Hall, the Pointer Sisters and Jeffrey Osborne. And Spud played the piano—for Michael Jackson. He has no fear.

Our next game was against the Cincinnati Bengals, in Los Angeles. They'd gone to the Super Bowl in January; they were our conference champions. I ran for 126 yards—in the first half. I ran for two touchdowns—in the first quarter. I went 7 yards for one touchdown, and almost every Bengal on the field had a shot at me, and then I went 92 for the other and nobody even touched me. "My grandmother could have run that play," I told the media after the game.

What I meant was that the run was nothing special, I just did what I was supposed to do. My blockers opened up a big hole, and when that happens, my job is just to run through it as fast as I can and head for the goal line, and that's what I did. When I got to the end zone, I celebrated by shooting off a pair of imaginary six-shooters. Everybody else was out of breath, and panting, and I was going, "Bam, bam, bam," and I didn't feel the least bit tired. You never do, after a touchdown, not till you get back to the bench. Then you die.

My 92-yard run was the longest in the history of the Raiders, breaking my own two-year-old record by a yard, and was only the fifth run of 90 yards or more in the NFL in a quarter of a century. I had two of the five. We beat the Bengals for our third victory in the four games I'd played.

I was having fun, enjoying playing, enjoying winning and enjoying my teammates. It's strange, but the two Raiders I'm closest to are both defensive guys, Howie Long and Bill Pickel, and I guess it's just because we're the three baddest guys on the team, Howie, Bill and Bo, not always in that order. They're both funny, and Pickel is a black guy trapped in a white guy's body. He talks like a black guy and he calls all the other white guys "honkies." Howie's problem is that he went to a girls' college called Villanova. I know it's a girls' college by the way Howie talks. He never stops talking. He would be all right if we could put a muzzle on him. But it's great to have two friends you can talk to about anything and not have to worry about them repeating it to anybody.

Steve Smith, our fullback, has no brains. Anybody who hits linebackers the way he does can't have any brains. He just loves to block. He loves to block the meanest guys that ever strapped on a helmet. He hits guys and the ground shakes, and he opens holes for me, and I love him for it. He does what he does so that I can have a great game, and that makes him feel good. He's the most unselfish player I've ever seen.

Steve Wisniewski was just a rookie in 1989, and he's still a kid in a man's body. He's big, but he's gentle. He hasn't yet learned the killer instincts you need in professional football, but he will, and he's going to be awesome. With him blocking at one guard and Max Montoya at the other, I don't have to worry about guys catching me from behind. Those two guys will protect me, and I won't have to worry about anything except running.

I'll just mention a couple more. Willie Gault is a great athlete. He made the Olympic team in 1980 as a sprinter and in 1988 as a bobsledder, and he's the only guy on the Raiders who's beaten me in a fair race. When he was a senior at Tennessee and I was a freshman at Auburn, I think he beat me by a step in the sixty. But I like to remind him that we beat Tennessee in football my freshman year. Willie is a country boy who's got new teeth and a new smile and wants to lead the Hollywood life. He's a real nice guy.

So is Tim Brown, who won the Heisman Trophy two years after I did. He's a cool dude, and quiet, more mature than people think, but he likes to party on Thursday nights, which is "Camaraderie Night." All the players that want to meet at a certain bar, then go from bar to bar, just getting to know each other better, I guess. I go home and get to know my family better.

After the Cincinnati game, we had a 5–4 record and we were starting to think about the playoffs. We wanted it for us, and we wanted it for Art Shell, because he is just what a head football coach should be. I don't think there's a player on the team who has mixed feelings about Art. I think everybody likes him. He's played the game, he knows the game, he knows the mentality of athletes, he knows what we have to do in practice and what we don't have to do. He doesn't have us out on the field for three-hour practices. We go out, we do what we have to do until we get it right and we get the hell off.

Art's an up-front guy who lets you know what he thinks and tells you that if you have a problem with anything he's doing, come to him and tell him about it, don't sit around and gossip about it. He's an honest guy.

I had my third straight 100-yard game against San Diego, but our little winning streak came to an end. I just missed breaking away for another touchdown run of 90-plus yards. If the Chargers' safety hadn't reached out and grabbed my left foot, I would've been gone—and we would've won the game.

Then I got pounded pretty good by Houston—didn't do much against them—and we lost our second in a row. I wasn't much help the next two weeks, either, against New England and Denver, but we won both of those games, and we had a 7–6 record with three games to go and a reasonable chance for the playoffs.

Marcus Allen returned for our next game, against Phoenix, and he scored the winning touchdown—I had another 100-yard game—and our record was 8–6. All we had to do was win our last two games, both on the road, against Seattle and the New York Giants, and we would definitely be in the playoffs. Even if we just won one of the last two, we'd probably be in the playoffs.

We lost both.

We should've beaten Seattle. We lost by six points and I had a touchdown taken away from me. On fourth and goal, I dove over the top, just like I did against Alabama in college, and I came down short, but I was still on my feet. I stretched out and stuck the ball across the goal line. It was a touchdown. I broke the plane of the goal line. You could see it on all the television replays. But the officials said I didn't score and gave the ball to Seattle, and we lost, 23–17. If I scored on that dive—like I did to beat Alabama, 23–22—we would've beaten Seattle, 24–23.

The next week, we stayed with the Giants for a while, and then they whipped our asses in the fourth quarter. It was cold, but it was just as cold for them as it was for us.

I only needed to gain about 80 yards in each of the last two games to go over 1,000 for the season, but I didn't come close. I finished the year with 950 yards rushing, averaging 5.5 yards a carry, the third-best average in the NFL.

I don't put much faith in numbers, but my rushing average for the Raiders after parts of three seasons in Los Angeles was 5.3 yards a carry, which put me ahead of the career averages for Jim Brown, O. J. Simpson, Eric Dickerson, Gale Sayers, Walter Payton and Herschel Walker. I'm not saying that I'm better than all of them, or even any of them, but at least I was in good company.

Shortly before the end of the season, NBC Sports announced that they had learned that Bo Jackson was going to be giving up football in 1990. They hadn't learned that. They hadn't learned anything.

I had too much fun playing football *and* baseball in 1989 to give up either of them. If I tried to stop, it'd be like asking a guy who'd been smoking for fifty years to stop, cold turkey. I'm an addict.

Besides, even with football and baseball, I still had time at the end of the year to go back to school, to go to Auburn and work on the credits I needed to graduate. I wasn't going to be a quitter. I wasn't going to let down my mom.

For one of my classes, I made a seven-minute video on what it's like to be a student in Auburn's School of Human Sciences. I produced it, I wrote it and I narrated it.

I don't like doing just one thing.

First he scratched his spikes in the dirt of the batter's box. Then he scratched his crotch. He was ready. He glared at the pitcher, cocked his bat, waited for the delivery. The pitch came in, and he swung, and he missed.

Furious, he grabbed the handle of the bat with one hand and the barrel with the other, lifted the bat and slammed it across his knee.

"Owwww!" Billy Crystal hollered. "Owww! That hurt!"

Bo Jackson began laughing.

Crystal, ex-college ballplayer decked out in a big league uniform, raised the bat once more and once again cracked it over his knee. The bat remained intact. The knee buckled. Billy staggered.

Bo fell. He started rolling on the artificial turf of the infield at Royals Stadium, doubled up in laughter.

The bat was supposed to break easily. The bat was pre-sawed. It was supposed to be as fragile as a toothpick. But Billy cracked the wrong part of the bat over his knee and, instead of imitating Bo, he had devastated Bo. "I ain't laughed so hard in a long time," Bo said.

Billy and Bo, the comic and the comet, had met at Royals Stadium, several hours before game time, to tape a segment for *Comic Relief,* the annual HBO special hosted by Crystal, Robin Williams and Whoopi Goldberg for the benefit of the homeless in America. Nike contributed shoes and cash to *Comic Relief;* Bo contributed his presence, and his sentiments.

"There are people out there," Bo said, "who see the way we live—we live like kings—and they don't have a roof over their heads or any idea where their next meal is coming from. I like being able to do something for them."

The pairing was a delightful one, the actor who had dreamed up *the* catch phrase of the '80s—"You look mah-velous"—and the athlete who had inspired *the* catch phrase of the '90s. Bo knows comedy. "I knew Billy was funny," Bo said. "I'd seen him on TV. But I didn't know he was such a little sucker. He's a Smurf."

Crystal was staggered again. That hurt more than the bat.

"But he's a good ballplayer," Bo said. "You see him taking ground balls at third base? He knows what he's doing."

Crystal felt better.

"He's got a big heart," Bo said.

Crystal stood ten feet tall.

"Take a look at my stance," he said.

Billy stepped into the cage again, using a different bat, and swung and hit a ground ball.

"What should I do?" he asked.

"Don't poke your ass out too far," Bo suggested. "And keep your eye on the ball."

Bo grinned. "That's what they always tell me, anyway," he said.

They got along beautifully, Billy and Bo, a two-man mutual admiration society. Billy asked baseball questions, and Bo offered comic answers.

Crystal wondered if Bo would describe the confrontation between pitcher and batter, the essential conflict of baseball. Bo captured it eloquently.

"I don't hear the crowd, I don't hear the cheering," Bo said. "I get in the batter's box, and I say, 'It's me and the pitcher and if he lays one down the pipe, I'm going to shoot it right back up the pipe. I'm gonna try to take his balls off with it.'"

This time, Crystal cracked up. He recovered sufficiently to pitch a question about the feeling of hitting a home run, and once again Bo connected. "Don't look up at the ball," he said, "unless you know you've hit it to East Hell."

Crystal was as impressed by Bo's gift for words as he was by Bo's gift for games.

Later, after the game, relaxing in a Mexican restaurant with George Brett, Billy asked Bo, "Which is harder, baseball or football?"

And Bo said, "Speaking a sentence. Speaking a sentence. That's what harder."

8

IN MY NEXT LIFE, I WANT TO BE A DOLPHIN—OR AN F-16

I rolled over and opened one eye and saw the clock on the table next to my bed. The time was a little after six-thirty. I jumped up and ran to the window. It looked to me like the sun was starting to go down. The game at Fenway Park was supposed to have started at six o'clock. I reached for my clothes with one hand and for the phone with the other. I pressed "O."

"May I help you?" the hotel operator said.

"Excuse me," I said, "but what time is it?"

"It is six thirty-seven."

"I know this may sound stupid," I said, "but is it A.M. or P.M.?"

"It's A.M., Mr. Jackson," the operator said. "You can go back to sleep."

I couldn't.

I never had more trouble sleeping than I did during the spring and summer of 1990. I couldn't fall asleep at night. I couldn't stay asleep in the morning.

Right from the start of the baseball season, we were losing and losing and losing, and I lay awake trying to figure out how we could've won, what I could've done to help us win.

I hate losing.

I watched movies till three or four in the morning, and then stared at the ceiling, or dozed off for a while, then stared at the ceiling some more, till it was time to watch the soap operas. I watched "One Life to Live," "All My Children," "Guiding Light." I knew all the characters as well as I knew my own family.

I was sleeping three, four, maybe five hours a day.

Losing was eating at me.

We weren't supposed to be losing. We were supposed to be one of the best teams in baseball. Some people picked us to finish first in the American League West, to beat Oakland, the defending world champions. On paper, we had an unbelievable pitching staff. We had Saberhagen, Gubicza and Gordon, who had won 55 games among them for the Royals in 1989. We had Storm Davis, who had won 19 games for Oakland, and Mark Davis, who had saved 44 games for San Diego. Saberhagen had won the 1989 Cy Young Award in the American League, Mark Davis the 1989 Cy Young Award in the National League. No team had ever had the two latest Cy Young winners on its staff at the same time.

We had half a dozen guys who had hit .300 in the major leagues—Brett, Wilson, Seitzer, Pat Tabler, Danny Tartabull and Gerald Perry. We got Perry in a

trade with Atlanta. I liked him a lot; he was somebody
I could really talk to. We had two guys who had
averaged more than twenty-five home runs a season
for the past three seasons—Tartabull and me.

We had Jim Eisenreich, who was named the
Royals' Player of the Year in 1989 when he batted .293
and stole twenty-seven bases. Jim is a good guy, quiet,
a hard worker who overcame a nervous disorder and
beat the odds and became an outstanding big league
baseball player. We call him Ice, and The Ice Man, and
sometimes Shake 'n Bake, which may sound hard to
people who don't understand baseball nicknames.
There's no prejudice to it, no cruelty; it's just to show
that we know what he's been through, and we admire
and like him.

We also had a couple of veterans, good leaders,
Frank White and Bob Boone, Smooth White and Papa
Boone, one almost forty and one over forty, guys who
could still play and could help out young players.

We had everything—and everything went wrong.

First we had the lockout, which delayed the start
of spring training and of the season. The lockout was
stupid. The argument wasn't really over money; there
was plenty of money for both the owners and the
players. It was over ego and power—the ego of the
owners, the power of the union.

The lockout didn't hurt me at all financially. In
fact, it helped me. It gave me time to make some
commercials and a few appearances. But I wanted to
be playing ball. It was time to play ball. I was running
out of things to do. I even went and bought a turkey
gun and arranged to go home to Alabama and go
turkey hunting for the first time the week they settled
the lockout. I had my plane tickets and my new gun
and my bags packed, and then the lockout ended, and

I kissed Linda and the kids and went off to Orlando and started working out. The family joined me a few days later.

I don't know whether it had anything to do with the short spring training, or whether it was because so much was expected of us, but once the season began, first our pitching was horseshit, and then our hitters were horseshit, and we spent almost the entire spring in last place in the American League West. I was horseshit, too.

I struck out too many times. I didn't hit enough home runs. I didn't drive in enough runs. I made too many errors. And every now and then, when I did something stupid, like swing at a ball over my head or in the dirt when we really needed a hit, I cracked another bat over my knee. I didn't want to break bats. I really wanted to tear up the whole stadium, turn it upside down, run everybody out of the stands. I wanted to go in the dugout and throw a bat or a helmet or the water cooler—anything to get rid of the frustration.

Sometimes I just wanted to go back to the bench and cry.

I kept hearing rumors that the Royals were going to trade me, and as much as I liked the city and the fans—most of them—I started hoping they would. I didn't want to be anyplace where they didn't want me. I was hoping they'd trade me to a team where I could come back and beat the shit out of them and laugh in their faces. But I was willing to be traded to anyone except the New York Yankees. I'd retire from baseball before I'd play for George Steinbrenner.

I was hurt, and I was angry.

I wasn't happy with the way the Royals had been treating me, right from the beginning of the year. We went to war over my salary. They had paid me

$610,000 in 1989. We went to arbitration in 1990. They offered me $1 million. I asked for $1,900,001.

I could've compromised, and asked for $1.4 million or $1.5 million, and maybe gotten it, but I asked for what I thought I was worth, no more and no less. I'm not saying $1 million isn't a lot of money—it is—but Mark McGwire, Fred McGriff and Ruben Sierra were all in situations similar to mine, and all of them got *raises* of more than $1 million in 1990, all of them got *salaries* of $1.4 million or more. Sierra got a raise of almost $1.3 million.

They'd each had a little more than three full seasons in the big leagues, just like me, and they'd each had statistics similar to mine in 1989. They beat me in some departments. I beat them in some. Like me, they were eligible for arbitration for the first time. Of the three, Sierra was asking for the highest salary— $1.9 million—so I asked for one dollar more. I'm not saying that I'm a better ballplayer than Sierra or McGriff or McGwire, but I know one thing. I sell more tickets.

In 1989, the Royals had the highest home attendance in their history, and the highest road attendance. I certainly wasn't the only reason, and I may not even have been one of the two or three main reasons, but I did have something to do with it. All during the year, for weeks before we came into a city, teams kept promoting the fact that Bo Jackson was coming to town. Maybe fans came to watch me strike out; maybe they came to boo me. Or maybe they came to see me hit a home run; maybe they came to cheer me. But they came. Nike and AT&T and Pepsi-Cola aren't stupid. They wouldn't use me in their commercials unless they figured that people wanted to see me.

I lost in arbitration. They say in baseball you're no longer a virgin once you go to arbitration and lose, once you hear the ball club that pays your salary, that urges you to do your best, argue against you, tell an arbitrator why they think you're not worth much, why you're overrated. I listened. During the season, the Royals tell me to swing away, to drive in runs, to go for the long ball, not to worry about the strikeouts, but in arbitration, they say Bo strikes out too much, he doesn't make contact, he kills rallies. They even denied that I sold more tickets. It makes it hard to know when to believe them.

Richard Woods discussed with John Schuerholz the idea of the Royals offering me a multiyear contract, but Ewing Kauffman, the co-owner of the Royals, said no. Mr. Fogelman was having financial problems with some of his other investments, so he was no longer the more active co-owner, Mr. Kauffman was. I had always liked Mr. Fogelman, even when he was surprised and hurt by my desire to play football.

My $1 million salary made me only the tenth-highest-paid player on a team with a $24 million annual payroll, the highest-paid team in baseball. We had two pitchers with contracts promising them more than $3 million a year, and we had three other players earning more than $1.5 million a year. All of them were getting more than George Brett, which was flat-out ridiculous.

For sixteen years, George had been the best player on the Royals, twice the American League batting champion, thirteen times a member of the All-Star team. For him to be only the sixth-highest-paid player on the team made no sense. No more sense than it made for me to be the tenth-highest-paid. George and I were the black sheep of the Royals. We were not Mr. Kauffman's favorites.

The money itself wasn't what bothered me. What it showed about the way they felt about me was. I didn't dwell on it. I had more important things on my mind. My mother was sick. Linda's mother was very sick. And Linda was pregnant. The health of my family came far ahead of my salary.

I had a run-in with the manager early in the season. We were playing in Toronto, and Linda made the trip with me, because we had an off-day between Toronto and Milwaukee. We played the Blue Jays Sunday afternoon, and after the game, Linda and I were going to drive to Buffalo, where her mother was living. We both wanted to see her mother. She was a very special lady, and we didn't know how much longer she'd be with us. I was going to rejoin the team Tuesday.

We were losing on Sunday, and I made the last out in the top of the eighth inning, so I knew I probably wouldn't get to bat again. In the ninth inning, I sat in the dugout while our first two batters made out. One more out, and the game was over. I went down in the tunnel leading from the dugout to the locker room and watched the third out from there.

Then I ran for the locker room, stripped, showered, dressed and was on my way out to meet Linda within minutes after the game was over.

When I got to the ballpark in Milwaukee on Tuesday, Duke called me into his office and said, "It really looks bad to the rest of the team when you're already undressed when they get to the locker room."

I exploded. "Look," I said, "when my wife is out there waiting for me, and she's six months pregnant,

I'm always going to be the first one off the field and the first undressed and in the shower and dressed and out of here. I'm a team player on the field, but once we leave the field, I'm not gonna sit in front of my locker and cry over a loss. We got too many games for that. Off the field, my family comes first. If you're looking to use me as a scapegoat, you're barking up the wrong tree."

Duke knew I wasn't backing down. "You know," he said, "we're looking for you to be more of a leader."

"I don't want to be a leader," I said. "You got too many pussies on this team, too many babies. I don't have time for babies."

I meant it. I like most of the Royals, and I respect most of them, and I love some of them, but there are one or two I have real trouble getting along with. One, anyway. I'm not going to name him, but he knows who he is.

This is the kind of guy he is. One day I took my bow and some arrows into the locker room and set up a target right outside the bathroom door. A lot of the guys took turns shooting the bow. Everybody knew we were doing it, and if somebody wanted to go into the bathroom, we stopped and waited till the coast was clear.

This guy went into Duke's office and asked if he could use Duke's bathroom and Duke said, "Why?" and he said, "Because Bo is shooting arrows at the bathroom in the locker room and somebody could get hurt badly." So Duke sent John Mayberry, one of the coaches, out to tell me to stop shooting arrows in the locker room.

This guy is the kind of guy if other players have secrets that are supposed to stay in the locker room, he runs home and tells his wife and she tells the other wives. Maybe I should've wrung his neck when I had the chance a few years ago.

I had my annual confrontation with Saberhagen, too. One day I wore a brand-new pair of silk pants, a nice shade of tan, to the ballpark. I changed into my uniform and went out for early batting practice, and when I came back to the locker room, one of the clubhouse guys told me to take a look in the bathroom. I thought Saberhagen was probably in there with one of his practical jokes.

He was in there, all right, with my silk pants. He had them in the sink, with hot water running, and he was scrubbing them. He had been throwing fat juicy cherries at Storm Davis, and a few times he missed Storm and hit my locker and the cherries burst and stained my pants. He was trying to destroy the evidence.

The pants cost $205.

Saberhagen paid for them. I didn't whip his ass, because I knew he could afford it.

I like Saberhagen when he's not doing stupid things, I really do. I can't help it. I just like children.

━━━━━

I hate the pettiness, the jealousies, the finger-pointing that can get in the way of just playing ball. The game can be so much fun when you're winning, when you're loose, when you're fooling around with your teammates and with the fans in the stands. I love playing games with the fans. They're unbelievable.

In Boston, for instance, they hold up signs that say: BO KNOWS SHIT. That's one of the nicer ones. They try to take pictures of me and I hide my face behind my glove and they holler at me. In New York, they sing songs to me, like "Jackson takes it up the ass, doo-dah, doo-dah," and instead of getting angry, I smile and raise my hands like I'm conducting an orchestra. During one series in New York, when Eisenreich and Tartabull were both out with injuries, George Brett had to play the outfield, and the fans greeted him by yelling, "George Brett's wife is a dyke, George Brett's wife is a dyke." That was pretty damned stupid. George isn't even married.

I don't mind the fans getting on me. In fact, I like it—as long as I'm on the road. It doesn't sit well with me when fans boo their own players—whether it's me or anyone else. Up in Boston one game, Mike Greenwell struck out and they booed him like he had missed the ground ball Bill Buckner missed that cost them the World Series. Greenwell had hit .300 for three straight years for them, and they were booing him.

Even with all the losing in 1990, there were still so many good things about playing ball. I kept making more friends on other teams, guys I really liked. When the Minnesota Twins came to town, Linda and I invited Kirby Puckett and his wife to come to dinner. When the Oakland A's came in, I'd get together with Mark McGwire. (I also got to know Rickey Henderson with the A's. He's a nice guy, but if I ever open up a restaurant, I'm going to name a foot-long hot dog after him. I'll call it the Rickey Henderson with extra mustard. But he's a nice guy. We talk a lot.) I told Ellis Burks of the Red Sox that if any of his teammates wanted to use good weight equipment, instead of the junk they've got at Royals Stadium, they could come over to my house. I've got a great weight room down in my basement, and I never use it myself, except for the sauna.

On the field, I was glad that Duke moved me from left field to center field. I liked having all that room, the freedom to go thirty or forty yards in either direction and the feeling of being in charge, of controlling the outfield. I made errors, but I also made some good plays, running catches, diving catches, strong throws.

The throw I made against Chicago early in the season—I made the catch and bounced off the wall and turned and threw and doubled Carlton Fisk off first base—got a lot of attention, but to me, it was a horseshit throw. It was too high. I wanted to throw it on a beeline to first base. Still, we got Fisk.

I had other good moments. I stole home. Once, with the bases loaded, I fouled off a bunch of pitches till I drew a walk that forced in a run. I hit home runs that traveled more than 450 feet. Once, on an inside-the-park home run, I sprinted around the bases in 14.7 seconds, and when I came home, I didn't want to slide the way I usually do, bending my knee, because my knee was sore. So I decided to slide in on my ass, feet first, with both my legs straight. I lay back flat so that if the catcher took a swipe at me with his glove, he wouldn't hit me in the face. I guess I looked like those people on the little sleds in the Winter Olympics, the luge sleds. As I slid across the plate, I just sort of flipped myself up onto my feet, without using my hands, and the fans went crazy. It looked to them like I wasn't the slightest bit tired after racing around the bases. I gave my teammates five and went into the dugout. Of course once I sat down, I was winded, but the fans didn't see that. They thought I wasn't even breathing hard.

I suddenly got hot a couple of weeks before the All-Star break. In one stretch, I hit ten home runs in eighteen games, and I drove in more than twenty runs, raised my totals and my batting average to respectable levels. My spurt came too late to get me elected to the All-Star starting lineup—I finished fourth in the American league outfield voting behind Jose Canseco, Rickey Henderson and Ken Griffey, Jr.—and when Tony La Russa, the manager, decided not to choose me, even though he said I deserved to be on the team, I was glad. Linda was due to have the baby the week of the All-Star Game, and I was just as happy to spend a couple of days at home with her and with the kids.

I got into the All-Star Game anyway—into the telecast. Nike introduced its new cross-training commercial during the game, with Sonny Bono wandering through and with me playing about fifteen different roles: Bo the football player, Bo the baseball player, Bo the basketball player, Bo the hockey player, Bo the weight lifter, Bo the soccer player, Bo the cyclist, Bo the auto racer, Bo the surfer, Bo the golfer, Bo the caddie, Bo the tennis player, Bo the jockey, Bo the cricketeer, Bo the director—you name it. I even got to do a British accent. I thought it was the best commercial I'd done.

I don't really play all of those sports, not yet, but I will. I've never played an official round of golf, for instance, but I intend to. Right now, I play in the backyard, using Spud's plastic balls. I've hit real golf balls, but I haven't figured out a swing technique yet. I swing like I'm swinging a baseball bat. I can slice a · ball about 300 yards.

Somebody gave me a set of clubs in 1987, when we were living in an apartment complex outside Kansas City, with a big open field out back. I went out one day with my new clubs and Spud and a dozen golf balls. When I faced the field, there were some apartment houses on the left, a wide open area down the middle and woods on the right. I aimed the first ball down the middle and it sliced into the woods. I aimed the second ball down the middle and it sliced into the woods. I aimed the third ball down the middle. Woods again. I'm not dumb. I figured if I turned and aimed to the left, toward the apartments, then the ball would end up down the middle.

I aimed the fourth ball to the left and I hit it and, just as I figured, it sliced right down the middle. I teed up another ball, aimed to the left again and hit it right on the nose. The ball took off like a rocket. Absolutely straight. No slice. Right at the apartments. It hit something—*bam!* I picked up my tee, threw my golf clubs back in the bag, grabbed Spud and said, "C'mon, we're going back inside."

We went back in our apartment, but my conscience was killing me. I took Spud and we got in my truck and rode around to where I hit the last golf ball. I saw a camper up there, behind the apartments, but I couldn't find my ball, and I couldn't spot a broken window anywhere. If I'd found one, I would've confessed and paid for it. But since nobody was out looking around, and I didn't see any shattered glass or anything, I just went back to my apartment.

Other sports?

I'm a pretty good diver. When I was playing minor league baseball in Memphis, all the players lived in one of Mr. Fogelman's apartment complexes, and we had a swimming pool with a diving board. Mike Miller and Jere Longenecker and I used to have diving contests almost every day. Mike would always win because he could do flips and twists, and I would always come in second. At Auburn, I used to dive off the ten-meter board by the pool, and sometimes, on Saturdays, we'd get a boat and go up the lake to a place called Chimney Rock. We'd climb up to the top, maybe sixty or seventy feet high, and dive from there into the lake, the way people dive off the cliffs in Acapulco. I also water-ski and I scuba dive. I'm a water person.

I have no desire to be a boxer—I've punched people, but never in a ring—and none to be a basketball player. Pat Williams, the general manager of the Orlando Magic, actually offered to sign me and let me play in an NBA game—for a minute or two, anyway—but I figured I'd leave that to Charles Barkley and Chuck Person and the other Auburn basketball players who used to run and hide from us football players.

I do think I could be a good soccer goalie, a decent tennis player, a professional cyclist and a competitive auto racer—if I ever decided to make those sports serious hobbies. The one sport I do intend to try soon, on a world-class level, is bobsledding.

In the first place, the timing for the Winter Olympics is perfect; I can fit it in between the Super Bowl and spring training. In the second, I think, with my speed and my strength, I could be the best bobsled pusher ever. I think my team could be the first ever to get a speeding ticket. And I love speed.

I'm not sure whether I should aim for the 1992 Winter Olympics in France or the 1994 Winter Olympics in Norway. I guess it depends on when I decide to give up football.

Right now, I have no plans to give up football—or to give up baseball. After all, it's not playing two sports that wears a person down; it's dealing with the media. I think I can survive that. But I am going to

have to start working harder on my physical condition-
ing to keep playing both sports. I may even have to
start lifting weights.

The last time I lifted weights regularly was when
I was a junior in high school. The only times I've lifted
since have been to treat specific injuries, to build up
damaged muscles. My idea of a good workout isn't
pumping iron. It's going hunting, bagging a deer that
weighs between two hundred and three hundred
pounds and dragging him out of the woods. Or going
fishing and fighting for an hour to bring in an eighty-
pound grouper or a two-hundred-pound jewfish.

I don't have any specific goals in football and
baseball, nothing that I feel I *have to* accomplish before
I retire. I don't think about the Hall of Fame in either
sport; it just doesn't cross my mind. I don't think about
setting records; I've always hated to study history, and
I don't much care about making it. I do know that I'd
love to play in a World Series, and in a Super Bowl,
because that's what everyone's aiming for at the start
of each season, and because those are two things I've
never done, and I love to do new things.

I know people are going to keep talking about
me, about what they think I could do, and what they
think I should do, and why I should give up baseball,
and why I should give up football, and I don't mind
them talking—when people stop talking about Bo,
that's when I'll start to worry—but the truth is they
don't know what the hell they're talking about. They
don't know what Bo's capable of doing if he concentrated on one sport because Bo doesn't know, either.

I think more guys are going to try to play two
sports professionally—and some of them won't be hot
dogs—but I think the owners are going to make it

more difficult by making the contracts more restrictive. That's too bad because I'd like to see guys like D. J. Dozier and Rodney Peete succeed in both sports. But it'll be tough.

When I decide to give up football, or baseball, or both, I won't have any regrets, and I won't miss it—as long as I'm the one who makes the decision, as long as I'm not *forced* to quit. I know I want to get out while I'm healthy. I want to get out with sound knees and a strong back. I want to be able to take my kids hiking and fishing and horseback riding and mountain climbing and camping. I probably won't go to a ball game unless Spud or Nick or Morgan wants me to take them. Then I'll go—for them. Otherwise, I'd rather take a boat out on a lake, or shoot my bow in the woods, or just work around the house, fixing things.

I want to help my kids grow up. I want to teach them to share their toys, even if they have a million of them, and I want to teach them to help and protect each other, and I want to teach them discipline. Linda and I set a time for their naps, a time for them to go to bed, and I see that they stick to it. They know that the living room, the dining room and the library are off-limits to them, and that if they go in there, I'll spank their butts.

I'm not a perfect father. Sometimes I lose it with the kids. Sometimes I go too far. When they start smacking each other, I threaten them: "I'm gonna take my bow and arrow and shoot you boys" or "I'm gonna lock you outside and freeze you into ice cubes and put you in my drink and drink you."

"No, you're not," they say, calling my bluff.

Then I pick them up and carry them out, and they start screaming.

I don't only threaten the kids. I threaten Linda, too. I keep telling her that when Spud turns twelve, I'm going to buy him a hooker for his birthday.

"You better not do that to that boy!" Linda says.

And I tease her and tell her, "I'm quite sure he'll like it."

I'm not going to push any of my children into playing sports if they don't want to, but I think they'll want to. They don't have to play football or baseball. In fact, I'd rather see them play golf and tennis. I'd love for Nick to be the next Boris Becker.

I want to spend more time with all of my family, not only my wife and my children. When I stop playing football, I'm going to invite all of my brothers up to watch the last week of the baseball season and then I'm going to take them all hunting, maybe up in Montana or Alaska. Jerry and Anthony and I are already hunters. Ronald and Clarence, they just hunt women. We're probably going to have to teach them how to look through a scope.

One of the things I'm going to do for myself is get a pilot's license and buy a P-51, a Mustang, one of those great World War II fighter planes with the Rolls-Royce engines. I've read books about the Mustang, and someday I'm going to own one and fly it myself.

Another thing I'm going to do is work with children. I'm not sure exactly how. Maybe Linda and I will set up some kind of center for children, where she can use her training and I can use my experiences, my feelings.

I have messages I try to get across to kids. Whenever I speak to them, I say, "Look, I've tried drugs, I've tried drinking, and I've found that my body doesn't function well if I do that, it just doesn't work for me. I can't speak for all of you, but I know that if I had kept using drugs or drinking, I wouldn't be where I am now. I get high on sports, I get high off nature, off streams and woods and blue skies, and I think that's the best way to get high."

I might like to have a children's television show of my own. I'd call it something like "Bo's Miracle Factory." Strictly kids on the show. No parents. I'd talk to the kids, and I'd listen to them. I might try to teach them some things, and I'm sure they would teach me some things. Each week I'd make a kid's wish come true. I'd like to be able to do that, make a wish a week come true.

I have a few wishes of my own.

When I die, I want my tombstone to say: HERE LIES A BALLPLAYER.

And when I come back, I want to be reincarnated as a dolphin—or as an F-16.

But I'm not ready to go, not yet. I still have too much to do, too much to learn.

I've already learned some things.

I've learned that I can get on my bike and ride and ride and ride and never come to the end of the earth.

o Jackson looked straight into the camera and sang:

> Wubba wubba wubba wubba
> Woo woo woo,
> Wubba wubba wubba
> And a-doodly-doo

Now Bo was into it, caught up in the song, pumping his arm, like a cheerleader.

> He went wubba wubba wubba
> And I sang along.
> Yes, wubba wubba wubba
> Is a monster song!

Bo finished with a flourish, firing his fist in the air, and the director, the technicians and even a Muppet or two burst into applause.

Clearly, Bo Jackson's debut on "Sesame Street" was a success.

Bo had a huge grin on his face. He had not exactly *sung* the lyrics to "The Monster in the Mirror." He had lip-synched them. He had mouthed the words soundlessly. Even before the cameras started to roll, he had warned the small audience crowded into the "Sesame Street" studio, "Bo don't know music."

Bo did know waists, however. When one of the wardrobe people brought in a pair of football pants for him to wear, Bo just glanced at them and said, "Lineman's pants. Too big."

The wardrobe man seemed skeptical. He looked at the slender waist on the pants, looked at the sturdiness of Bo and suggested, "Try them on."

"Don't have to," Bo said. "Give 'em to me."

Bo took the pants, squeezed about five inches of waist line between his thumb and his forefinger and said, "Cut this much out." The wardrobe man went out shaking his head. He came back ten minutes later with the altered pants, and Bo pulled them on. They fit perfectly.

Then Bo went out to do his bit for "Sesame Street." He was one of many celebrities who had been asked to sing backup to Grover, the furry blue Muppet for whom Christopher Cerf and Norman Stiles had written "The Monster in the Mirror." Chubby Checker, who had started a dance craze called The Twist before Bo was born, preceded Bo on the "Sesame Street" set; the actress Tyne Daly followed Bo.

But while the others only sang, Bo also performed. In one scene, he sat down in a sandbox with two children, filled his football helmet with sand and said, "Full." Then he dumped out the sand and said, "Empty." In another scene, he tapped three children on the head, one at a time, and said, "One, two, three." He handled his lines flawlessly.

Finally Bo shared the stage with Bo Peep and her flock. She greeted him, "Bo, you don't know Peep," parodying the Nike ad, and then proceeded to introduce herself.

Bo, in turn, introduced himself to her sheep. He stuck out his hand and said, "Bo."

The first sheep replied, "Baa."

"Bo."

"Baa."

"Bo."

"Baa."

There is room for Bo to work his way up to Shakespeare.

When Bo was finished, he shook hands with everybody, posed for pictures with Chubby Checker, Bo Peep and some people who use their real names, then signed autographs and went back to his hotel. He had one hour to rest before he had to go to Yankee Stadium to play baseball. Even though he had arisen early, after a night game and no more than four hours' sleep, Bo wasn't able to nap, wasn't able to fall asleep. He went up to Yankee Stadium tired and testy.

Bo is almost always testy in New York. He does not feel comfortable in the city. He gets an attitude. He becomes even more intimidating than he usually is.

He put on his uniform, took batting practice and sat down in the Kansas City dugout. Whenever a reporter came near him, bearing a tape recorder or a notebook and a quizzical look, Bo growled, "What do you want?" He was playing a game. He wanted to see if he could scare the reporters away. He could.

But, shortly before the game, Bo's attitude changed. He softened when Brian Newton, a thirteen-year-old, and his sister Brooke, who is ten, and their parents came to meet him in the Royals' dugout.

"Hey, dude, what's happening?" Bo asked Brian, who had come from Chillicothe, Ohio, to fulfill a dream, to meet

Don Mattingly and Bo Jackson. Brian's trip had been set up by a group called A Special Wish Foundation, which tries to fulfill the dreams of youngsters with life-threatening disorders. Brian Newton was suffering from a form of cancer called Ewing's sarcoma.

"Where you sittin'?" Bo asked Brian.

The youngster indicated the box seats behind home plate.

"I'll try to wave to you during the game," Bo said.

Bo signed a fistful of baseball cards for Brian. He enjoyed signing for Brian. Bo knows when autographs mean something. This was the second time Bo had helped turn A Special Wish into a reality; the organization has asked Bo if he would become their national spokesman.

The game began, and Bo came up in the first inning, two men out, George Brett on first base. Bo looked into the stands behind home plate. They were crowded now, and he could not spot Brian. But Brian saw Bo and cheered for him.

The Yankee pitcher, Andy Hawkins, got ahead of Bo, one ball and two strikes. "Oh, no, here we go," Bo thought, angry because he was one strike away from a strikeout. He knows, with his swing, that he will strike out often, but, still, he hates to strike out. "You have to swing at anything close," he told himself.

Hawkins threw a pitch that wasn't close, evening the count at two-and-two, then came back with a fastball on the inside part of the plate. Bo swung and connected and muscled the ball deep to center field. The Yankees' center fielder, Deion Sanders, spun and scrambled back toward the wall.

Sanders, like Bo, is a major league baseball player and an NFL football player. They are the only two men competing at that level in both those sports. Sanders is still new at it. He is a defensive back for the Atlanta Falcons who calls himself Prime Time, and permits others to call him Neon Deion. He loves to flaunt his jewelry and his wealth, and he revels in the limelight. His crackers do not sit well in Bo's bowl of soup.

Sanders leaped. He could have saved his energy. The ball sailed over the fence at the 408-foot mark, a two-run home run. "I couldn't believe it," Brian Newton said. "I had just met him and he hit a home run."

Two innings later, Bo came up again, once more with Brett on base. Bo knew that Hawkins wouldn't give him an inside fastball again. Bo was looking for a ball on the outside part of the plate, and Hawkins threw the first pitch on the outside part of the plate. "Right in my zone," Bo said. Bo hit the ball 464 feet, the longest home run of the season in Yankee Stadium. The ball landed deep in the bleachers in right-center field. Sanders saved his energy.

"Two home runs!" Brian Newton said. "I couldn't believe it!"

In the fifth inning, Bo came up for the third time, with Brett and Kevin Seitzer on base and Hawkins still on the mound. Stump Merrill, the Yankee manager, went out and talked to Hawkins.

Hawkins's first pitch to Bo was two feet outside. Bo and everyone in the ballpark presumed that Merrill had told Hawkins to pitch to Bo, but not to give him anything he could possibly hit.

"I knew he wasn't going to throw me another fastball," Bo said, "I was looking for doo-doo."

Hawkins delivered a slider, outside, off the plate, but not a very good slider and not far enough off the plate. Bo swung, hardly a classic swing, a perfunctory swing. "I wasn't trying to hit it out," Bo said.

He got a piece of the ball, no more. He lifted a pop fly to right field, a high pop fly, a routine out—except that the ball kept going and going and going.

Bo didn't look at the ball. He looked at Jesse Barfield, the Yankees' right fielder. When Barfield stopped running for the ball and started looking at it, Bo knew the ball was going to clear the right-field fence.

The ball landed three rows back in the stands.

Nobody could believe it.

Bo had three home runs and seven runs batted in—both feats tying the Royals' record for a game—and it was still only the fifth inning. He would almost certainly come to bat at least twice more.

Bo Jackson was on the brink of baseball history. Only nine men in more than a century of major league baseball had hit four home runs in a game. No one had ever hit five.

He circled the bases, recorded the one hundredth home run of his brief career, hugged the teammates who were waiting at home plate and slapped the hands of the Royals who were celebrating on the dugout steps. Then he sat down and, as the cheers thundered through the stadium, the Yankee fans transformed into Bo fans, exhilarated by his performance and hopeful of witnessing history, Bo's thoughts suddenly shifted away from baseball.

He thought of his mother-in-law, Linda's mother, Amanda.

Amanda Garrett had died the previous week. She had died a few days before Linda was due to give birth. The funeral was scheduled to be held in Thomasville, Alabama, not far from Mobile, the day after Linda's due date. Linda, of course, wanted desperately to go to her mother's funeral, to say goodbye, but in her ninth month, she could not risk a commercial flight.

Bo hired a Learjet. He was on the road with the Royals, so he had the jet pick him up in Boston the day before the funeral. Then he flew to Kansas City and picked up Linda, and together they flew on to Mobile. The pilot carried a special map that indicated the sites of hospitals along the route between Kansas City and Mobile. "If Linda went into labor," Bo said, "we could land right away."

The flight went smoothly. Bo and Linda drove to Thomasville, spent the night, then drove to the funeral the next day. During the services, Bo's lips moved with the preacher's. He knew the prayers, the passages from the Bible, by heart. He had spent so many Sundays in church.

Linda found consolation in the fact that her mother's suffering had ended and in the fact that she was able to get to the funeral. Still, her anguish was considerable, and so was Bo's. He loved Linda's mother almost as much as he loved his own.

After the funeral, Bo and Linda reboarded the Learjet and flew back to Kansas City. Bo paused long enough to see Spud and Nick, who had stayed home with their baby-sitter. Spud didn't want Bo to rejoin the Royals in Boston. "I have to," Bo said.

"Mommy," Spud said, "Daddy doesn't love us any more."

Bo knew that Spud didn't mean it, but still the words stung. He assured Spud that he loved him and Nick and their mother. Then, reluctantly, Bo got back on the rented jet and returned to Boston. He had been gone barely thirty-six hours.

Three days later, Bo hit three home runs in his first three times up against the Yankees and remembered his mother-in-law and vowed that he was dedicating the three home runs to her, and if he got them, the fourth and the fifth, too.

Bo didn't get to bat again.

In the bottom of the sixth inning, Deion Sanders hit a line drive to right-center field, and Bo, racing toward it, thought he could catch the ball if he hurled his body through the air, if he dove as though he were attacking Alabama's goal-line defense.

Bo flew, his body horizontal, three or perhaps four feet off the ground. He challenged gravity. He stayed airborne for five or six yards. But the line drive kept slicing away from him, and when he realized the ball was going to get past him, he tried to twist his body in midair, to change direction, to start chasing after the ball. "My butt got higher than my head," he explained. Instead of hitting the ground flat, spreading the impact from head to toe, Bo hit with his upper body first, from the rib cage up. As he crashed, he felt the breath rush out of him. He felt the left shoulder *pop.*

"I wasn't aware of the grass or the ball or the stadium or anything," Bo said. "I didn't hear the crowd. I didn't know that Deion scored. It was like I had a vision. I saw a picture—of my shoulder. I clearly saw the ball and the socket, and I saw the ball come out of the socket."

His left shoulder was dislocated. His left arm went numb. The right fielder, Pat Tabler, ran to him and said. "C'mon, Jax, get up," and Bo said, "I can't, Tabby, I can't." With Tabler's help, Bo managed to push himself up, and as he did, he felt the ball slip back into the socket in his shoulder. But now in his mind all Bo could see was the injury he suffered in the Texas game in his junior year in college, the injury to his right shoulder.

"No, no, no," he thought. "I don't want to have surgery. I don't want to miss the rest of the season."

He wasn't thinking about a fourth home run, or a fifth. He was thinking about seventy-four games still to play. The Royals were in their eighty-eighth game, and Bo had nineteen home runs and fifty-seven runs batted in, a pace that, over a full season, would produce thirty-five home runs and 105 runs batted in, handsome figures, far more than respectable. He was batting .270. He was the hottest hitter in the league. And he was hurt.

"Should we get Willie up?" Mickey Cobb, the trainer, asked.

"You better," Bo said.

He trotted off the field, and when he reached the dugout, he stood on the steps and stretched, and the shoulder popped out again. Bo swung his arms and coaxed the shoulder back in. Then he went into the locker room and, more in anger than in pain, he exploded. He kicked over a garbage pail. He threw a stool. He pounded a table. He paced back and forth, fuming, furious with himself, with his body, for allowing himself to be injured. He was so angry he almost forgot the pain.

Finally he permitted the trainers to look at him. He calmed down sufficiently for the Yankees' doctor to examine him. "I don't think you have a total dislocation," the doctor said. But he sent Bo to the Columbia Presbyterian Medical Center for X rays.

"I was in a lot of pain," Bo said, "until they wheeled in a guy who'd just been hit on his motorcycle and dragged for a block. His skull was crushed. His legs were broken. All of a sudden, I didn't hurt any more."

But Bo had fluid in his shoulder and a slight tear in a muscle. He was not going to need surgery, but he was going to need rest. He had to put his left arm in a sling. Three days after the injury, Bo went on the disabled list for the third time in three seasons.

The next morning, Bo was awakened by Linda at a quarter to six. "Vincent, I think my water broke," she said.

Bo was in a fog. "What, what?" he mumbled.

"I think I'm in labor," Linda said.

Bo shook himself awake. He jumped up and rushed to his closet and began pulling out clothes. He skipped the sling. He drove Linda to St. Luke's Hospital in Kansas City.

Shortly after noon on Saturday, July 21, 1990, Linda gave birth to Morgan *Amanda* Jackson. Bo and Linda had decided a few days earlier that Morgan's middle name should be Amanda, after Linda's mother, not Vincentia.

Once again, Bo watched his child being born, and once again he was fascinated and overwhelmed by the miracle. Once again, he was in love.

Morgan Amanda Jackson's statistics were as awesome as any of her father's home runs. She weighed in at nine pounds, ten ounces.

Bo went to the ballpark that night armed with cigars, his chest puffed out. He told everyone how big Morgan was, and how beautiful. He couldn't stop bragging.

"Damn, Bo," Gerald Perry said, "is she walking yet?"

Then Bo went home and changed into a sparkling outfit for Linda, beige slacks and an aqua silk shirt. On his way to the hospital, he bought a box of fried chicken to share with his wife.

It had been raining most of the day.

Bo parked near the hospital and, as he walked from his car, a white Chevette raced by, straight through an enormous puddle. The splash drenched Bo.

He walked into his wife's room, carrying fried chicken,

soaking wet. Linda had just finished breast-feeding the infant. She was cradling Morgan in her arms, talking to her, kissing her. Bo saw them together and smiled. He had his two women now, and his two boys, and his two sports, and it didn't matter if he were wet and wounded. Nothing could dampen his happiness.

The child who was filled with anger had grown into a man who was filled with joy.

BO'S CAREER—IN STATS

BASEBALL BO

AUBURN

Year	G	AB	R	H	Avg.	HR	RBI	SB	SO
1983	26	68	14	19	.279	4	13	5	34
1985	42	147	55	59	.401	17	43	9	41
1986	21	69	21	17	.246	7	14	5	30
Totals	89	284	90	95	.335	28	70	19	105

MEMPHIS

Year	G	AB	R	H	Avg.	HR	RBI	SB	SO
1986	53	184	30	51	.277	7	25	3	81

KANSAS CITY

Year	G	AB	R	H	Avg.	HR	RBI	SB	SO
1986	25	82	9	17	.207	2	9	3	34
1987	116	396	46	93	.235	22	52	10	159
1988	124	439	63	108	.246	25	68	27	146
1989	135	515	86	132	.256	32	105	26	172
Totals	400	1432	204	350	.244	81	235	66	510

FOOTBALL BO

AUBURN

REGULAR SEASON GAMES

Year	G	Att.	RUSHING Yds.	Avg.	TD	LR	No.	RECEIVING Yds.	Avg.	TD	LP
1982	11	127	829	6.5	9	53	5	64	12.8	0	43
1983	11	158	1213	7.7	12	80	13	73	5.6	2	44
1984	6	87	475	5.5	5	53	4	62	15.5	0	21
1985	11	278	1786	6.4	17	76	4	73	18.3	0	29
Totals	38	650	4303	6.6	43	80	26	272	10.5	2	44

BOWL GAMES

Bowl (Yr., Opponent)	Att.	Yds.	Avg.	TD
Tangerine (Fr., Boston College)	14	64	4.8	2
Sugar (So., Michigan)	22	130	5.9	0
Liberty (Jr., Arkansas)	18	88	4.9	2
Cotton (Sr., Texas A&M)	31	129	4.2	2
Totals	85	411	4.8	6

L.A. RAIDERS

Year	G	Att.	RUSHING Yds.	Avg.	TD	LR	No.	RECEIVING Yds.	Avg.	TD	LP
1987	7	81	554	6.8	4	91	16	136	8.5	2	23
1988	10	136	580	4.3	3	25	9	79	8.7	0	27
1989	11	173	950	5.5	4	92	9	69	7.7	0	20
Totals	28	390	2084	5.3	11	92	34	284	8.4	2	27

ACKNOWLEDGMENTS

I want to thank Arthur Kaminsky and Richard Woods, the New York lawyer and the Alabama one, for making the marriage between Bo and me. I want to thank David Gernert of Doubleday for making the marriage work. I want to thank Janet Pawson, Arthur Kaminsky's aide, and Susann McKee, Richard Woods's aide, for their help and encouragement. I want to thank David Housel and Mike Hubbard from the Auburn sports information office, David Rosenblatt from the Auburn University Archives and Dean Vogelaar and Steve Fink from the Kansas City Royals public information department. I want to thank Mark Thomashow and his Nike associates. I want to thank Jay Hill for gathering background material and Al Braverman for gathering photographs. I want to thank Joanna and Jeremy Schaap, my college-age children, for transcribing many of the tapes of my interviews with Bo and for comments and suggestions. I want to thank Trish Schaap, my wife, for reading and rereading and offering the insights of someone who cares little for sports, but a great deal for people. And, mostly, I want to thank Bo Jackson for being candid, for being accessible and for being Bo. It was easy to get Bo to talk about his mother and his wife and his children and his childhood. It was hard to get Bo to talk about his touchdowns and his home runs. Bragging is not his sport. Which is why it was my idea, not his, to incorporate the tributes from his teammates George Brett and Howie Long and the briefer comments from baseball and football experts who have watched Bo at play. Bo doesn't think what he's done is so great. I, respectfully, disagree.

—DICK SCHAAP
1990